POSITION
yourself for
SUCCESS

To: JENNIFER

With Thanks & Appreciation

God Bless You

12/21/18

POSITION YOURSELF FOR SUCCESS

GOD'S WAITING TO DO WONDERS
THROUGH YOU

Ruthven J. Roy

REHOBOTH
PUBLISHING

Rehoboth Publishing
P.O. Box 33
Berrien Springs, MI 49103

For additional copies of this book visit:
www.rehobothpublishing.com
www.networkdiscipling.org

To:

Lyris,

my precious wife, and our daughters,

Charisa
Lyrisa
Mirisa

Table of Contents

Acknowledgment

Saying thanks can sometimes seem so trite because of its natural common usage in everyday life; but I cannot think of a more appropriate word to convey my sincere gratitude to God and my Family—my wife, Lyris, and daughters, Charisa, Lyrisa and Mirisa—who are always there to support and encourage me. Also special thanks to Emmerson Cyrille, Patricia Elder and Dr. Ermine Leader, for their valuable contributions that added the finishing touches to this manuscript, making it reader-friendly and ready for production.

Introduction

What is true success? How should one really measure it, and against what standard? What may be considered successful by one person or by one criterion, may be regarded as a total failure by another. In our world, success is generally measured by wealth and fame, materialism, glitz and glamour. However, we are so often shocked by the behind-the-scene reports of the pain and misery associated with the lives of so many people whom the achievement gurus have labeled "successful."

Somehow, it seems that these tangible elements of achievement alone are sadly insufficient instruments to measure what characterizes a truly successful and satisfying life. The wise preacher aptly describes this heartbreaking dilemma in Ecclesiastes 2:1-11. According the Bible, there is *good* success and there is also *bad* success—that is, success that is really failure from God's perspective. Listen to what the wise preacher says of Him:

For to a person who is good in His sight He has given wisdom and knowledge and joy, while to the sinner He has given the task of gathering and collecting so that he may give to one who is good in God's sight.

Ecclesiastes 2:26

Here we see that it is God's perspective of one's life that really determines if that person is a success or failure. Let me illustrate this through two powerful, divergent examples:

> *Now Joseph had been taken down to Egypt; and Potiphar, an Egyptian officer of Pharaoh, the captain of the bodyguard, bought him from the Ishmaelites, who had taken him down there. <u>²The LORD was with Joseph, so he became a successful man</u>. And he was in the house of his master, the Egyptian.*

> Genesis 39:1, 2

The Bible called Joseph a successful and prosperous man even though he was a slave in Potiphar's house, and later, in Potiphar's jail. Materially, all Joseph had was the clothes upon his back and the visible signs of his bondage. Moreover, the text says that Joseph was successful because **God was with him**. In my estimation (and I know that I am supported by the Word of God), this solitary statement—*God was with him*—is the immovable center-piece of what determines whether or not a person's life would be one of *good* success, or absolute failure.

Additionally, this empowering declaration of God's presence with Joseph, the slave boy, is repeated three times in the very first chapter of this captivating narrative. See

Genesis 39:21, 23. It also forms the backbone for every experience Joseph encountered along the path to his very successful life in a foreign land.

One may be quick to ask: "But isn't the presence of God with everyone?" In a general sense, yes, otherwise all humanity would have been dead a long time ago. However, God's presence is His constant, graceful act of mercy, until individuals are brought into His full favor by the experience of salvation through our Lord and Savior, Jesus Christ.

> **It is God's presence in your life that really brings about "good" success.**

Whenever this experience occurs for you, the presence of God, through the indwelling Holy Spirit, is not only with you, but also within you (John 14:16, 17). It is this indwelling presence of God that makes all the difference in the world, in the immediate, and residual outcome of a person's life. It is God's presence in your life that really brings about *good* success. The Word of God declares:

that "... *the eyes of the LORD move to and fro throughout the earth <u>that He may **strongly support** those whose heart is **completely** His</u>*"

(2 Chronicles 16:9)

When God is supporting you, failure is never an option. Often what appears as failures are God's stepping-stones, paving the way for you to achieve greater and better things. Now, let us take a quick look at the flip-side of the Joseph narrative—that is "success" that is not good. Jesus gives us an example of this type of success in the gospel of Luke. He said:

> "*The land of a rich man was very productive. *[17]*And he began reasoning to himself, saying, 'What shall I do, since I have no place to store my crops?' *[18]*Then he said, 'this is what I will do: I will tear down my barns and build larger ones, and there I will store all my grain and my goods. *[19]*'And I will say to my soul, "Soul, you have many goods laid up for many years to come; take your ease, eat, drink and be merry."'* [20]*But God said to him, 'You fool! This very night your soul is required of you; and now who will own what you have prepared?' *[21]*So is the man who stores up treasure for himself, and is not rich toward God.*"

> Luke 12:16-21

The downfall of the rich man was the result of the confidence he placed in himself, his shrewd business expertise, and his "ability to predict" his own future. Pay very close attention to how many times he used the personal pronouns "I" and "my"—"I" x 6 and "my" x 5. He was at the center of his "success." This very intelligent and competent businessman is a working definition of "bad" success. Essentially, this understanding of "success" is based predominantly on what "I" have planned, what "I" have decided, what "I" have done or achieved and what "I" have amassed for myself. There is absolutely very little or no room for God in the self-driven individual who is in the pursuit of the successful life.

It is this preoccupation with the self that lends to the deceitfulness of the human perspective of what success really is. Such success is generally appraised by the fleeting elements of this earthly realm, which are wholly inadequate to measure the total life of a person. Jesus stated very clearly that a person's life—success or failure—cannot be measured by his materialistic abundance or lack thereof.

"Watch out! Be on your guard against all kinds of greed; a man's life does not consist in the abundance of his possessions."

Luke 12:15, NIV

Thus, there must be more to success in this life other than one's material possessions. This book is about the achievement story of a man called "Joshua," who God promised *good* success if he would position himself in obedience to His will. What is even most interesting is the fact that Joshua's life serves as a mirror in which we are able to see the reflection of our own life story.

You are about to begin a very exciting journey that will stir your deepest emotions, pry your most intimate thoughts, destroy your inhibiting fears and open new windows for a fresh vision of achievement and success in your life. God is not just your heavenly Father way beyond the blue. He is your lifelong Counselor and Friend right here and now. He wrote the success story of your life long before you arrived on this planet, and is now waiting for you to step into the storyline He has written for you.

My frame was not hidden from You, When I was made in secret, And skillfully wrought in the depths of the earth; [16]Your eyes have seen my unformed substance; And in Your book <u>were all written the days that were ordained for me</u>, <u>when as yet there was not one of them</u>.

Psalm 139:15, 16

Notice, God knew you (verse 1), wrote your destiny and the days He ordained for your life, long before your arrival in the delivery room where you were born. Such knowledge is so high, it's mind-boggling, and no one could attain it (verse 6). *His thoughts are not our thoughts; neither are our ways His ways. For as the heavens are higher than the earth, so are His ways higher than our ways, and His thoughts than our thoughts* (Isaiah 55:8, 9). Every life on this planet has a divine purpose, but very few have realized their true potential and destiny, because the position strategies they have chosen for their lives do not harmonize with God's perfect plan for them. God, Himself said:

"For I know the plans I have for you," declares the LORD, "plans to prosper you and not to harm you, plans to give you hope and a future."

Jeremiah 29:11

This very resourceful book offers you the enviable opportunity to re-position yourself for *good* success. Your pre-ordained destiny awaits your presence, O child of God. Rise up, move forward, and embrace it now! God is waiting to do wonders in and through you.

CHAPTER 1

This is God:
May I have Your Attention?

"Moses My servant is dead; now therefore arise,
cross this Jordan, you and all this people, to the land
which I am giving to them, to the sons of Israel."

Joshua 1:2

*J*oshua and all the children of Israel were in deep mourning over the death of their beloved leader, Moses. For thirty days they were weeping and lamenting in the plains of Moab (Deuteronomy 34:8), as they remembered and rehearsed all their marvelous experiences associated with Moses' leadership since they left Egypt. Although they knew that their aged prophet and leader was quickly approaching his death, when it did finally occur, they were completely devastated. When the stark reality of his absence did set in, and the silence of the wilderness was no longer punctuated by his commanding, spirit-filled voice, a strange and foreboding emptiness pierced the souls of the wailing multitude.

The distraught people suddenly became acutely aware of how much they really did love Moses, despite the numerous occasions they wanted to get rid of him. What a fickle multitude of ex-slaves they were! Even while Joshua understood and accepted God's commission to be the new leader to replace Moses (Deuteronomy 31:23), he could not detach himself from the gripping sadness of that very tear-jerking occasion. Although Joshua had received the official endorsement of Moses in the presence of the people, through the laying on of the prophet's hands, he probably felt stuck in the lingering waves of emotions that had overcome the people.

God remembers the past, but does not live in it.

It was during this period of emotional numbness that the God of Israel and of Moses suddenly appeared to Joshua. He was possibly at a loss with regard to where to begin in executing his new role as Israel's leader, and with how to motivate them to move forward to possess their inheritance. While he was thus engaged, waiting patiently to get Israel's full attention, God was ready to direct his. He too had been waiting to perform wonders through Joshua.

The Bible says that God spoke to him, saying: *"Moses My servant is dead . . ."* This was not only a statement of confirmation about the death of Moses; it was also a declaration of finality. There was no going back to Moses, although he was God's faithful servant and had done many wonderful works on His behalf before the people and against foreign nations. God remembers the past, but does not live in it. He is the great I AM, the ever-present One.

Consequently, God first had to lift the dark cloud of sadness that had engulfed Israel, and that had momentarily stymied the enthusiasm of His servant, Joshua. However, once God had gotten his attention, He immediately gave Joshua his marching orders. God's first command called for swift action; He expected a prompt response: *"Now therefore arise. . ."* The "therefore" links the present to the past, and has the reference to the dead prophet, Moses.

In other words, "he who is dead, is dead, Joshua!" *"Now therefore arise!"* God had been grooming His servant, Joshua for this very moment from the time Israel begun it journey through the wilderness (Exodus 33:7-11). He is the One who promotes men and women to positions of greatness for His own purpose. Joshua's unshakeable confidence in the words of Jehovah, amidst the faithless, oppositional cry of an angry multitude which was, at any moment, ready to stone him and Caleb, had singled him out as a man great faith and courage.

⁶Joshua the son of Nun and Caleb the son of Jephunneh, of those who had spied out the land, tore their clothes; ⁷and they spoke to all the congregation of the sons of Israel, saying, " The land which we passed through to spy out is an exceedingly good land. ⁸If the LORD is pleased with us, then He will bring us into this land and give it to us— a land which flows with milk and honey. ⁹Only do not rebel against the LORD; and do not fear the people of the land, for they will be our prey. Their protection has been removed from them, and the LORD is with us; do not fear them." ¹⁰But all the congregation said to stone them with stones. Then the glory of the LORD appeared in the tent of meeting to all the sons of Israel.

Numbers 14:6-10

Joshua had distinguished himself before Moses and the congregation of Israel as a man who could be trusted to carry out all of God's commands. He was also a very faithful servant and follower of Moses over the forty years of Israel's journey through the wilderness. That's a very long time to walk humbly, but faithfully, in the shadow of one's predecessor.

It was Joshua who accompanied Moses up the mount to receive the Ten Commandments (Exodus 24:13), and never once turned away from his leader's side. Joshua had learnt quite a lot from just being in the presence of the only prophet (beside Jesus) that ever walked the face of the earth who knew God face to face (Deuteronomy 34:10). He was such a loyal understudy of his master, that by the time of Moses' death he was a very seasoned, God-fearing leader, characterized in the Word as one who was filled with the spirit of wisdom (Deuteronomy 34:9).

> **God is the One who promotes men and women to positions of greatness for His own purpose.**

In spite of the very sad circumstances that surrounded him, Joshua was fully ready to assume the leadership of Israel when God called on him. Thus, God could forthrightly and confidently say to His servant: *"Arise!"* "It's time to move out," (my paraphrase). *"Cross over <u>this</u> Jordan, you and all <u>this</u> people."* This was Joshua's moment to shine in a totally different capacity. He was no longer the servant who waited on the directions of his leader, Moses. He was now the leader who waited on directions directly from the God of all the earth. It was now his responsibility not only to represent God before the people of Israel, but also to represent the people before God; and to cooperate with Him in leading the nation to its promised destiny.

As one carefully reads the account of God's call on Joshua to replace His faithful servant Moses, it is not very difficult to notice the distinguishing adjective "this" that qualifies both the Jordan and the people of Israel. These identical qualifiers beckon our inquiry and understanding. *THIS* Jordan is a very clear indication that there was something quite unusual about the Jordan at the time of Israel's impending crossing. At this place, and at this time, the Jordan overflowed its banks, on account of the melted snow from the mountains of Lebanon.

The springtime phenomenon forced excess water to pour into the Jordan in torrents, making it gravely unsafe for anyone to cross, let alone a teeming multitude of undisciplined ex-slaves—infants, children, the aged—with all their animals and belongings. *THIS* Jordan presented an evacuation nightmare, more serious and life-threatening than that precipitated by the infamous hurricanes "Katrina" and "Ike," which devastated many gulf cities in southern United States in 2005 and 2008 respectively.

"*THIS* Jordan" was not the only major challenge facing the newly appointed leader of Israel. Shepherding *THIS* weary, impatient and rebellious people was an equally very daunting task. However, God commanded Joshua to take the responsibility of handling both. "*THIS* people" carries the connotation of quite an inglorious history that began in the clay pits of Egypt and that haunted the children throughout their forty years of wandering in the desert. It was "*THIS* people" who murmured against God from the gates of Pharaoh's Egypt to the borders of the Promised Land.

THIS was the people who quarreled with Moses for water; railed on him for the flesh pots of Egypt; forced Aaron to make them a golden calf for a god; incited a mutiny against Moses and was ready at any moment to rebel against any new instruction he'd receive from God. *THIS* was such a cantankerous multitude of ex-slaves that God associated their volatile, unpredictable disposition with the waters of the raging Jordan that was overflowing its banks. Joshua was commissioned to take "*THIS* people" across "*THIS* Jordan."

God of Hope

"For I know the plans that I have for you," declares the LORD, "plans for welfare and not for calamity to give you a future and a hope."

Jeremiah 29:11

Despite Israel's selfish, rebellious, and reckless ingratitude, God, through His servant Joshua, offered *THIS* people the promise of a much brighter future. He instructed His servant to cross the Jordan and to take the ungrateful people along with him to the land that He was going to give to them. Because of His unconditional promise to His friend, Abraham, God was going to bring the patriarch's downtrodden, desert-worn descendants to their undeserving inheritance. Through His covenanted promise, God had already established His plan to give the sons of Abraham a glorious future, filled with bright hope. Consequently, His command to Joshua was to escort them to the place He had made ready for their possession.

You and Your Jordan

Crisis Intervention

Gaining a person's undivided attention is often a very difficult and challenging task when life appears to be good, and everything seems to be going according to plan. This is especially true when that individual is in a phase of life that is fulfilling a particular pleasure quest. During that phase, a person can become so absorbed in his activities and preoccupations that he is oblivious of other major events that may be occurring in his little world. Moreover, pleasure quest activities can lead a person to more addictive behaviors, from which the individual often feels quite powerless to break free.

How do we get the attention of someone caught in such a cycle, to focus on making a decision to change the course of events in his life? Social psychologists characteristically use an approach called "crisis intervention," in which they create a life-threatening crisis for the victim caught in the cycle of abusive behavior. Such a crisis has the effect of awaking and grabbing the victim's attention long enough for him to accept therapeutic treatment designed to rescue him from his unhealthy, destructive conduct.

> **Moses' death, prior to Israel's entrance into Canaan, was a God-appointed "crisis intervention" strategy.**

At the time of Joshua's appointment as the new leader of Israel, the people had been through cycles of abusive behavior toward God and His servant Moses for a period of forty years. The entire journey through the wilderness was a checkered history of whining, complaining and disaffection.

On the very borders of the Promise Land, when the spies returned with their reports, the stiff-necked people kicked off their final rebellion against Moses. They were quite ready to stone Caleb and Joshua to death for bringing back what they thought was a contrary description of their intelligence-seeking expedition. Had not this same Moses interceded for Israel, God would have wiped out the entire nation at the border; but He chose, instead, to destroy all those who were twenty years old and above (Numbers 13, 14).

However, Israel had been down that road before when they witnessed the rebellion and destruction of Nadab and Abihu (Leviticus 10), and of Korah, Dathan and Abiram (Numbers 16). Nevertheless, these very compelling incidents did not stop all their bitter complaining and revolting against

God's appointed servant. Consequently, Moses' death, prior to Israel's entrance into Canaan, was a God-appointed "crisis intervention" strategy, not only to inject fresh leadership into *this* unbroken nation of intolerant ex-slaves, but also to provide new direction for Israel's grand and exciting future.

God was now using the very one (Joshua), whose faith embraced the divine vision of Israel's future, to lead a nation in crisis, out of its rebellious, complaining debacle, into an era of conquest and final settlement. It took the crisis of Moses' death to be the launching pad for this new experience. The death of this faithful servant of God, along with the prior wasting of the people twenty years of age and older, were symbolic of the death of the old cycle of the wilderness life of the nation. Something new was about to occur and the crisis in the plains of Moab (Moses' death) was the precursor to this impending event.

Sometimes God, in His mercy, has to break through our "this-worldly" preoccupations in order to fulfill His design and purpose for our lives. We can become so engrossed in the things of this age that we completely lose our focus on God, or we place Him on the back-burner because of all that is "cooking" in our self-absorbed lives. Jesus' warning to the people of our age is:

> *"And take heed to yourselves, lest at any time your hearts be overcharged with surfeiting, and*

drunkenness, and cares of this life, and so that day come upon you unawares"

Luke 21:34

John also cautioned:

[15] *"Love not the world, neither the things that are in the world. If any man loves the world, the love of the Father is not in him.* [16]*For all that is in the world, the lust of the flesh, and the lust of the eyes, and the pride of life, is not of the Father, but is of the world.* [17]*And the world passeth away, and the lust thereof: but he that doeth the will of God abideth for ever."*

1 John 2:15-17

A worldly heart is one that is so crowded with the demands of this life that there is very little room (or none at all) or time for God and His will in the daily experience of a person categorized by such a disposition. In such a heart, the love of the things of the world has supplanted the love of the

> **Sometimes God has to break through our "this-worldly" preoccupations with a crisis in order to fulfill His purpose for our lives.**

Father, and the person possessing that overcharged spirit belongs to the self-centered, "last-day" crowd who loves pleasure more than God (2 Timothy 3:5).

Therefore, quite often, God has to penetrate the thick crust of our blind, ambitious souls by precipitating crisis situations in our lives, in order to bring us to our divinely-appointed destinies. These crises help to jolt us into the reality of our human frailty, and to focus our attention on our desperate need of a power much higher than ourselves and our earthly assets. That power, we soon realize, is God Almighty. Invariably, in the center of our crisis, amidst our pain, suffering, sorrow and tears, the God of our fathers suddenly appears and gently whispers through the inner man of our spirit: *This is God: May I have your attention?*

Who or What is dead, is dead

The crisis God chooses to get our attention could be short and decisive, if we understand, receive and follow through on His instruction or revelation. It can also be long and protracted, which is a mere reflection of the time it takes us to learn the lesson God is trying to teach us. Moreover, crises often persist because we have a very difficult time letting go of the past, especially if it holds cherished memories and accomplishments, or unresolved brokenness and pain. However, in either case, crises are designed to put to death our cherished attitudes, behaviors, relationships, life-styles and dreams, so that new life and thoughts of God's ordering can emerge.

When God intervenes, He does so to change our perception of reality concerning our life and situation, and to give us brighter, clearer vision of things pertaining to our appointed future. Through the Spirit's enlightenment, we are able to identify and separate our old mental framework from the new revelation of God's will for our lives; but there still remains the challenge of making the choice to pursue the path that God has chosen for us.

> **Crises are designed to put to death our cherished attitudes, behaviors, relationships, life-styles and dreams.**

In this regard, the experience of Israel, prior to the nation's crossing of the Jordan, is very instructive for us. We cannot live our present and future lives by repeating what we did in the past. Moses, the great leader, was dead and there was absolutely nothing that Israel could do about it. After thirty days of weeping and wailing, of reminiscing and lamenting over their leader and their past, God had to bring the people to the realization that what was dead, regardless of its stature, had to be buried and left behind. A glorious future was ahead of them, but in order for them to inherit it, they had to let go of the past—so should we.

Wake up and smell the coffee

Many people fail to achieve meaningful success in their lives because they remain anchored to their past, instead of using old experiences as reference points to chart new directions to a rewarding future. It was while all Israel remained emotionally paralyzed by the death of their "larger-than-life" leader, that God blindsided Joshua with the command: "Arise!" In other words, "wake up and smell the coffee, Joshua!" "There is no more life in the past; you are no longer a servant of what is dead in your life. It is time for you to take the reins of leadership and move forward."

In a very similar manner, we cannot dwell in the past by reliving it every day, no matter how glorious or how dismal it may have been. Although it may feel great reviewing and rehearsing past achievements, and altogether dreadful, remembering past woes, **they are gone!** We must wake up, arise, and "smell the coffee." We must ask God for spiritual discernment and understanding to be able to identify and confirm what He has pronounced dead in his life, and resign it to the past.

> **You are no longer a servant to what is dead in your life.**

Not only must we know what is dead; but we must

also possess the wisdom and courage to bury what is dead—that is, we must come to terms with, and add finality, to it. Sometimes we try desperately to put new life in old fires—situations, friendships, failures, mistakes, love affairs, broken dreams—and end up with major conflagrations and disasters. Spiritual and natural wisdom dictate that we should "allow sleeping dogs to lie," and dead dogs to remain buried. We should not go about unearthing what is dead; the stench may be more than we may be prepared to handle.

God is the great I AM, the ever-present One. While the Almighty remembers the past, He always operates in the present. The psalmist David says that our God is a very present help in the time of trouble (Psalm 46:1). Through our afflictions and trials, the ever-present God is positioning us, His children, for divine intervention. By His circumstantial ordering we must put to death that which needs to die in our lives, and to bring about an altogether "new thing" of His own choosing. He says, through the prophet Isaiah, *"Do not call to mind the former things, or ponder things of the past. Behold, I will do something new, now it will spring forth; will you not be aware of it? I will even make a roadway in the wilderness, rivers in the desert.* (Isaiah 43:19, NASB).

However, in order to bring about a "new thing" into our lives, God often has to put to death that which is old. Quite frequently we resist such a change because we have grown so accustomed to the cycle of expectations from that which is old and ready to die, or from that which is already dead. In conjunction with this, the enemy of our souls influences us to magnify our fears—fears of our situation and our future—above and beyond our faith in the Almighty, who is able to do exceedingly abundantly above all that we could ever ask or think (Ephesians 3:20).

It really does not matter what your current situation may appear to be, or what you may be experiencing physically or emotionally. God already has a solution and a plan for your state of affairs. He can most certainly give you new directions in the midst of your chaos and confusion, and He is able generate new life in whatever appears to be dried up, decaying or dead in you. He is willing and able to make a way where there is no way—*a roadway in the wilderness* and *rivers in the desert*. Trust Him!

Crossing Jordan

As was cited earlier, the Jordan that confronted the children of Israel was not the typical, quiet stream that watered the valleys at the foot of Mount Lebanon. It was a raging torrent of melted snow and ice that rumbled relentlessly down the mountain gorges, overflowing the river's banks and strategic crossing-points. This made crossing extremely dangerous because Jordan's normal flow was violently disrupted. However, to cross over was a must, not only because Israel's future destiny lay on the other side, but because God Almighty, who is the security of the nation's future, had ordained the prompt crossing of the river.

Just like the experience of the children of Israel, a raging, formidable Jordan may be churning over before you, separating you from your life's dream or future destiny. Jordan does not only represent a great obstacle in your path to progress or to your destiny. It also symbolizes your meeting place for a miraculous encounter with God.

Your Jordan could be anything—a lingering illness or disability; a great loss—possibly of a loved one, your job or your home; a series of mishaps; severe economic hardship; a stalled job promotion; a disgruntled, vindictive co-worker, boss, neighbor or relative; a rebellious, wayward child; a cheating spouse or some other major challenge. Whatever you may be battling with right now, this thing has disquieted your spirit, has stolen your peace and joy, and has made you run the gauntlet many times over, with feelings of anger, fear, frustration, and fatigue.

Know this, dear child of God: Your Jordan is not just another obstacle in your path, but your God-appointed opportunity to qualify you for the next level in your relationship with Him and with others. *Every* Jordan in your life is your opportunity for spiritual, mental and emotional development, to make you a more resilient and resourceful person. However, your trouble and confusion stem from focusing most, if not all, of your attention and energies on your Jordan. This pre-occupation tends to blind your vision of your omnipotent Father who is constantly watching your every step and misstep. He is always working for you, and never against you. The apostle Paul reminds us all of the true nature of our Jordans. He says:

> [17]For our _light affliction_, which is but for _a moment_, worketh for us _a far more exceeding and eternal weight of glory;_ [18]While we _look not at the things which are seen_, _but at the things which are not seen:_ for _the things which are seen are temporal;_ but _the things which are not seen are eternal_.

2 Corinthians 4:18, KJV

Every Jordan presents an opportunity for spiritual growth and development.

Paul's first observation may come off as shocking to those who are going through the awful grind of their Jordan situations. He summarizes these as momentary and light. "Are you kidding me, Paul?" I can hear some of you saying to yourselves. But Paul is not kidding at all. He calls your situations and mine short-lived and light when compared to what they produce in and for us, as those relate to our eternal future existence. The veteran soldier of the cross of Christ also speaks to the matter of our focus. He appears to be saying that focus is everything whenever the believer is confronted with a Jordan experience. He says that the things that we see or perceive are temporary or changeable; but the things that we do not see or perceive are eternal.

What are those things that we do not see? Those are the things that pertain to the realm of faith—not only in God, but also in the promises found in His infallible Word. It is woefully difficult to focus on the problems associated with your Jordan and on the promises of God at the same time. Moreover, your breakthroughs do not come from looking at the Jordan, but on focusing on, and listening to, the God who allowed you to come to that never-before crossing. It is very important to understand that nothing just happens to any child of God, even if you did not start it.

> *Every* Jordan has a way through it before it begins to flow your way. That's heaven's guarantee!

Be assured that your heavenly Father is in the midst of your seemingly insurmountable situation, working out EVERYTHING for your good (Romans 8:28). He says: '*For I know the plans that I have for you,*' declares the LORD, '*plans for welfare and not for calamity to give you a future and a hope.*' (Jeremiah 29:11). The Word of God also promises that:

> *No temptation has overtaken you but such as is common to man; and God is faithful, <u>who will not allow you to be tempted beyond what you are able</u>, but <u>with the temptation</u> will provide the way of escape also, <u>so that you will be able to endure it</u>.*

1 Corinthian 10:13

There is absolutely no situation so trying that confronts you, of which God is not fully aware. The Bible makes it quite clear that Jordan-crossing experiences are not only the common lot of all humankind, but that God faithfully watches over all. He will not allow you to be tested beyond your ability to bear your trials, even though this appears inconceivable when you are going through your situations.

How often have you emerged on the other side of an ordeal you thought you would have never been able to handle, or even able to survive? Every Jordan has a way through it before it begins to flow your way. That's heaven's guarantee! With every temptation or trial, God has an ordained way of escape so that you would be able to bear and go through it. You have the unfailing assurance that if God has brought you to your Jordan, He is certainly able to take you through its raging waters triumphantly.

You have a secured destiny

*". . . cross this Jordan, you and all this people, to the
land which I am giving to them, to the sons of Israel."*

Joshua 1:2

In His instructions to Joshua, God commissioned the
newly-appointed leader to take His people across the Jordan
to the land that He had given them. Two things are
immediately clear from the above text—namely, (1) Joshua
was not going to cross the Jordan alone, and (2) God had
already prepared a place for him and the people. These two
very important details in this remarkable experience are
uniquely instructive for you as you position yourself for
success against your personal Jordan.

First of all, you must know and believe that crossing
your Jordan is never about you and you alone. God has
predetermined that your future success is tied to the destiny
of others. His blessings are never in isolation of those around
you. He never blesses you for yourselves alone. Whenever
you cross your Jordan, you will be a blessing to many others
on both sides of the crossing experience—those that are on
the side of Moab (trial) waiting to get over, and those on the
side of Canaan (destiny), who have already made it over.

Second, as a potential Jordan-crosser, you must also

know and believe that God has a future designed especially for you. He will most certainly bring you to it if you will only trust His wisdom and leadership instead of yours. You must have the abiding confidence that whatever is yours by divine design can never be taken away from you. No one, but yourself, can deter you from the future that God has established for you.

When you begin to believe and live by this truth, you will find your sense of peace and release from the harassment of your chaotic, wandering mind. It is only then you will begin to be aware of the divine presence, filling you with a feeling of hope and assurance. At that very moment of faith, you will be transported to a position of strength, where your mind will be more open to receive new insights and/or revelations from God. It is here that you will discover that there must be a clear path for you to negotiate your way right through your Jordan.

You may not know the way ahead, and the truth is you do not have to know the way. God, who has brought you to your Jordan, is the Way. He will take you through. When Job, the indomitable patriarch, was going through his Jordan, he left us these encouraging words:

⁹When He acts on the left, I cannot behold Him; He turns on the right, I cannot see Him. ¹⁰But He knows the way I take; When He has tried me, I shall come

*forth as gold. ¹¹My foot has held fast to His path; I
have kept His way and not turned aside. ¹²I have not
departed from the command of His lips; I have
treasured the words of His mouth more than my
necessary food. ¹³But He is unique and who can turn
Him? And what His soul desires, that He does. ¹⁴For
He performs what is appointed for me . . .*

Job 23:9-14

What this Jordan-crossing stalwart is saying in verses
9 and 10 above is that although he cannot fathom the ways
and moving (left and right) of the Almighty, he rests in the
fact that God knows the way he (Job) is appointed to travel.
He will bring him through on the other side of his Jordan like
refined gold. Because of this abiding confidence, Job was
steadfast in pursuing the following course of action: (1) He
never strayed from the path of righteousness, nor did he turn
aside from the ways of God. (2) He did not deviate from the
commands of God's Word, but treasured them more than his
necessary food.

> *1. You will never cross your Jordan alone.*
> *2. God has a future especially designed for you.*

What a sterling example for all potential Jordancrossers! In verses 13 and 14, Job gives us his experiential understanding of the Almighty, and these pointers we must never forget. (1) God is unique and we cannot bribe Him with our empty promises, or turn Him around from His purpose with our bitter crying. (2) Whatever God desires, He will do, regardless of how we feel about it, or of what we think about Him for doing or allowing it (Psalm 135:6). I know that this is a very hard one for many of us to deal with, but God's thoughts are not like ours, and our ways are absolutely not like His (Isaiah 55:8). (3) God will perform to the letter whatever His wise judgment has appointed for you and me.

Job's secret was that he surrendered himself completely to the will and the plan of God. He was determined to follow through on this commitment even if it meant losing his very life in the process. He declared with confidence, "*though He slay me, yet will I trust in Him*" (Job 13:15). This humble Jordan-crosser positioned himself for success and certainly reaped his reward on the other side of his harrowing experience. What does the Bible testify of him?

[10]The LORD restored the fortunes of Job when he prayed for his friends, and the LORD increased all that Job had twofold . . . [12]The LORD blessed the latter days of Job more than his beginning; and he had 14,000 sheep and 6,000 camels and 1,000 yoke of oxen and 1,000 female donkeys. [13]He had seven

sons and three daughters . . . ¹⁶After this, Job lived 140 years, and saw his sons and his grandsons, four generations.

Job 42:10-16

My fellow Jordan-crosser, God is waiting to do new things *in you* and *for you*. He declares

". . . I proclaim to you <u>new things from this time</u>, <u>Even hidden things which you have not known</u>. ⁷They are created now and not long ago; And <u>before today you have not heard them</u>, So that you will not say, 'Behold, I knew them.'"

Isaiah 48:6, 7

These things that God is about to do are quite new, and have never been thought of by you, or have never occurred before in your life. These things are new because God is creating them for you now. They are not from long ago. Therefore, you will never be able to say when it is all over, "I knew this was going to happen."

Through the experience of your Jordan, God is seeking to get your attention so that He can begin a new thing in your life. Are you even listening? Or are you, like Joshua

and Israel, preoccupied with groaning and moaning over
some perceived loss in your life? You are being positioned
for success. Are you ready for the journey? Your manual is
in your hand, so keep right on reading; and as you read,
remember God's promise through the prophet Isaiah:

> 2"*When you pass through the waters, I will be with you;
> And through the rivers, they will not overflow you. When
> you walk through the fire, you will not be scorched, Nor
> will the flame burn you.* 3"*For I am the LORD your God,
> The Holy One of Israel, your Savior ...*

Isaiah 43:2, 3

It is the common lot for all humanity to face major
Jordan crossings along the journey of life. However, you need
not be intimidated or overwhelmed by their threatening
waves. The Holy One of Israel, your Savior, promises that
those waters will not drown you, for He will be with you, to
take you right on through. Therefore, you can confidently say
to all your present situations: "Roll Jordan, roll; roll Jordan,
roll. Your threatening waves are nothing new, my Lord and I
will walk right through; so roll Jordan, roll" (the author).

CHAPTER 2

Platform Of Promises:
The Key To Success

³"Every place on which the sole of your foot treads, I have given it to you, just as I spoke to Moses. ⁴From the wilderness and this Lebanon, even as far as the great river, the River Euphrates, all the land of the Hittites, and as far as the Great Sea toward the setting of the sun will be your territory. ⁵No man will be able to stand before you all the days of your life. Just as I have been with Moses, I will be with you; I will not fail you or forsake you."

Joshua 1:3-5

*O*ne can only imagine Joshua's reaction as Jehovah began outlining what lay on the other side of the Jordan for him. Although he had been Moses' assistant for forty years, nothing could have prepared him or anyone else for a personal audience with the Almighty. Replacing Moses was already a larger-than-life responsibility, for the record says that *since that time no prophet has risen in Israel like Moses, whom the LORD knew face to face* (Deuteronomy 34:10).

Receiving commands from this revered servant of God was one thing, but obtaining such commands from the mouth of the Almighty, Himself, was something altogether quite different. The Bible does not tell us what Joshua's in-time reaction was during the divine visitation. It simply outlines what he did once the job interview was over.

A Very Firm Platform

Joshua left his "job interview" with great confidence because God had given him a very firm platform, which guaranteed the successful completion of his job prescription. The Almighty had established the foundation for Joshua's success, but it was up to him to operate from that base, or to establish one of his own choosing.

The framework of Joshua's platform was not made from the worthless materials of man's fleshly wisdom or good intentions. His was not like our current political platforms, which quite often make empty promises to the people during an election campaign, and renege on them when the election is over. No, a thousand times no! Joshua's platform was built upon the unfailing words of the Almighty God—words that cannot return unto Him void. He is the God who watches over His every word which proceeds from His mouth, to perform exactly what He says (Jeremiah 1:12).

God always anoints whomever He appoints.

It is very important to observe that God had already done the groundwork for laying down the platform that guaranteed Joshua's success. He had given Joshua a spirit of wisdom through the laying on of hands by His servant Moses. The Bible says that Joshua was filled with the spirit of wisdom (Deuteronomy 34:9).

God always anoints whomever He appoints, for without His anointing all other appointing is spiritually impotent. Men's anointing does not necessarily signify God's appointing; neither does their appointing imply God's anointing. However, God's anointing was the basis for Joshua's appointment as the leader to replace Moses, and without it, Joshua would have been only a footnote item in Israel's future.

It was God's appointing and anointing which formed the foundation of the platform for Joshua's service and future success, and His abiding promises were the sturdy framework which held the platform together. These promises were all grounded in the God of history, and evidenced in the life and leadership of His prophet, Moses. Hence, God made reference to His dead servant as He linked every promise He made to Joshua right back to his predecessor, Moses. He said to Joshua, *"Just as I have been with Moses, I will be with you"* (Joshua 1:5). In other words: "All the promises I made to your predecessor I have kept to the letter. I will do exactly the same with you. I will never leave you nor forsake you."

Joshua's platform of promises was held together by a consistent history of God's faithfulness. The Almighty is the God of His own word, for there is no higher authority beyond Him. Every promise and every word stops at Him, and there is absolutely nothing, and no one, that can get in the way of Him bringing to pass what He has spoken.

Every Place . . . I Have Given . . . to You

The very first component of Joshua's platform was God's promise of dynamic territorial expansion. He told Joshua that every place upon which he was about to tread on the other side of the Jordan was going to be his—exactly as He had told His predecessor, Moses. Notice, God did not set any limits to Joshua's treading. He could have trod all day long, in any and all directions for that matter. It made absolutely no difference. This was dynamic territorial expansion: You tread, you own. How awesome! Joshua's success as a real estate magnate was predicated on his ability to tread all over Canaan. God had already given all the lands on the other side of Jordan to him and the children of Israel. However, they had to tread on the land in order to own it. If they should stop treading for any reason—which,

PLATFORM OF PROMISES: THE KEY TO SUCCESS

incidentally, seven of the tribes temporarily did—they would only inherit where their feet had trod.

> **The dynamics of territorial expansion say:**
> **"You tread, you own."**

How did Joshua address the situation? He ordered treading scouts from each of the seven tribes, to walk through and describe their inheritance.

> *³So Joshua said to the sons of Israel, "How long will you put off entering to take possession of the land which the LORD, the God of your fathers, has given you? ⁴Provide for yourselves three men from each tribe that I may send them, and that they may arise and walk through the land and write a description of it according to their inheritance; then they shall return to me."*

Joshua 18:3, 4

This is a rather interesting improvisation to the original promise. Instead of allowing the people belonging to seven of the tribes of Israel to tread the land of Canaan, Joshua appointed three scouts from each of the tribes to do all the treading for them. In addition, these scouts were also required to write a careful description of the territory they covered for their tribal inheritance and bring it back for community assessment and validation.

Thus, the burden of the treading and the description of the territory were placed on the scouts, but the decision for ownership was placed on Joshua and the tribes. In any event, ownership was solely based on the territory covered by the treading scouts. No treading meant no territory! Little treading, little territory! Much treading, much territory!

Invincible Advance and Acquisition

Another fabric of Joshua's impregnable platform that positioned him for success was God's promise that no one would be able to stand before him all the days of his life. This was a major confidence booster and a life-time warranty in every sense of its definition. Joshua was guaranteed victory over anyone who would come up against him regardless of size, strength or material resources.

As Joshua and the people trod through territory after territory in the land of Canaan, God systematically dispossessed the inhabitants of the land in order to give it to the sons of Israel. They did not have to fight any legal battles to obtain their inheritance, because God was the One giving it to them. No man, system of government, or organization in the land was able to withstand the territorial advancement of the people of God.

In reflection of this unequal experience, Joshua wrote:

> [43]*So the LORD gave Israel all the land which He had*
> *sworn to give to their fathers, and they possessed it*
> *and lived in it.* [44]*And the LORD gave them rest on*
> *every side, according to all that He had sworn to their*
> *fathers, and no one of all their enemies stood before*
> *them; the LORD gave all their enemies into their*
> *hand.* [45]*Not one of the good promises which the*
> *LORD had made to the house of Israel failed; all*
> *came to pass.*

Joshua 21:43-45

It is crucially important to observe Joshua's understanding and eye-witness assessment of Israel's successful acquisition of, and settlement in, the land of Canaan. He said that the Lord *gave all* the land to Israel which He had pledged to their fathers. In other words, Israel did not earn or deserve the land. It was a gift to them because of God's promise to their fathers. The people did not only go in and possess the land, but also lived in it. What a testimony to God's faithfulness!

Additionally, God *gave* Israel rest from enemy

47

harassment on every side; for He *gave all* the enemies into their hands. Joshua was also very careful in pointing out that God's promises formed the immovable platform for Israel's ultimate success in Canaan. He said that *not one of the good promises which the LORD had made to the house of Israel failed; ALL came to pass* (Joshua 21:45).

Forever Faithful

Finally, God placed Himself on the line as He vowed to be with Joshua to the very end. He said: *Just as I have been with Moses, I will be with you; I will not fail you or forsake you* (Joshua 1:5). Experience was Joshua's great teacher. He was an eye-witness of everything God had done under the leadership of Moses. He saw the Red Sea part for the sons of Israel to walk right through, and saw it closed up again on Pharaoh and his mighty hosts. He felt the warmth of the pillar of fire during the very cold desert nights, and the cool shades provided by the cloudy pillar which protected the people from the punishing wilderness sun. He saw the manna which fell from the sky; the water which came from the rock; and the defeat of the Amalekites as Aaron and Hur held up Moses' hands.

Joshua knew first-hand Who was promising to be with him, and was confident of victory over any enemy, and success in any endeavor. He also knew that the God of Moses was a most faithful ally. He had a life-time warranty on a winning

PLATFORM OF PROMISES: THE KEY TO SUCCESS

ticket and that's all that mattered. History recorded the result. Here is Joshua's testimony in the closing days of his life.

> *⁹For the LORD has driven out great and strong nations from before you; and as for you, <u>no man has stood before you to this day</u>. ¹⁰One of your men puts to flight a thousand, <u>for the LORD your God is He who fights for you, just as He promised you</u> . . . He [I] gave you a land on which you had not labored, and cities which you had not built, and you have lived in them; you are eating of vineyards and olive groves which you did not plant.*

Joshua 23:9, 10; 24:13

Examine Your Platform

Find your purpose

This is such an amazing story; but, more importantly, this is not just Joshua's and Israel's story. It is a model of your story. As you confront your Jordan, be assured that God has an appointed destiny waiting for you on the other side of this challenging experience. There is not a life on this earth that is without some divine purpose. It is just simply very unfortunate that many people continue to live in hopeless

49

despair because they are either unaware or quite doubtful about this encouraging truth.

> **Whatever your purpose is in life, God has already given you the spirit of wisdom to fulfill it.**

The Joshua story serves as a powerful reminder of the reality of God's graciousness and favor to all mankind, but especially so to those who put their trust in Him. In His Holy Word He reminds us that *those who hopefully wait for Him [Me] will not be put to shame* (Isaiah 49:23).

Whatever your purpose is in life, God has already given you the spirit of wisdom to fulfill it. This is the solid foundation for your platform of promises which God has made available to you in His Word. These are His guarantees for your successful completion of your life's assignment. However, like Joshua, you have to disengage yourself right now from what is already dead in your life—past failures, self-appointed agendas, and unfruitful alliances, and the like—and move forward with God to inherit the new things that He has ordained for you and your household.

Therefore, seek the Almighty for wisdom, revelation and guidance regarding His purpose for you. Above all else, make His presence and His Word your daily portions. Why waste time, energy and your meager resources working outside the realm of your purpose? Seek God and His kingdom first and all other things will certainly fall into place (Matthew 6:33). Remember that no one but yourself is able to stop you from your God-appointed purpose. Find and establish it! This must be your first work.

Ignore or neglect it and you may find yourself back in your wilderness, wandering despondently around your barren mountain, strewn about with the dead carcasses of your failures, disappointments, fears, grief and pain. Always remember that it is in your appointment (or purpose) that you will find your anointing (wisdom and revelation) to make your life's strivings meaningful and effective.

Key to your success

Israel's victories over all her enemies, and her successful occupation of the territories of Canaan, were the direct result of God's faithfulness to all the promises He had made to his forefathers and to Joshua. This very firm, enduring platform became a beacon of hope and prosperity to all future generations of Abraham, including all believers in Christ. The Word of God promises that all who belong to Christ are Abraham's descendants and beneficiaries to all his covenant blessings (Galatians 3:29).

Therefore, do not base your success on frivolous or fanciful wishes, empty promises of men or baseless dreams. Experience has taught many of us that these approaches often lead to disappointing, painful results. How many continue to play cyclical games of "Russian Roulette" with their lives, hoping one day to hit the target they set for their future. The very fragile and unstable conditions of our present global environment and economies are very stark reminders that no earthly system is safe enough to guarantee a person's future success.

Many are currently living an unbelievable nightmare as they witness the ongoing failures of the private and public institutions they had trusted to protect their future investments and livelihood. These reputed vanguard organizations, purported as the protectors of the people's interests, are now seeking protection for themselves, as they experience the daily erosion of their once-thought-to-be immovable investment foundations.

Thank God, He holds the controls over all the situations that can ever arise in our lives. He can never be surprised by any emergency or disastrous eventuality. You can afford to stake your future success on the platform of His promises found in His infallible Word, and can be assured that not one of those promises will ever fail. The story of Israel and Joshua at the Jordan crossing speaks volumes to the life's situation of the average person, and you can adapt God's platform of promises made to Joshua as your very own.

All God's promises are solidly backed by His unfailing faithfulness.

The good news is that you can even choose to build your own platform with other precious biblical gems that speak directly to your Jordan situation. Once that platform is established on the Word of the Almighty God, and you choose to live by it, God will perform whatever He says in His Word. All His promises are solidly backed by His unfailing faithfulness. He once told His prophet Jeremiah, "*I am watching over my word to perform it*" (Jeremiah 1:12). Through His servant Isaiah, He also proclaimed:

> [10]"*For as the rain and the snow come down from heaven, And do not return there without watering the earth And making it bear and sprout, And furnishing seed to the sower and bread to the eater;* [11]*So will My word be which goes forth from My mouth; It will not return to Me empty, Without accomplishing what I desire, And without succeeding in the matter for which I sent it.*"

Isaiah 55:10, 11

You owe it to yourself, dear reader, to search His Word and locate His precious promises that He has spoken for your life, and then make the daily, unyielding decision to live by them in spite of all circumstances. It is much easier for your circumstance to fail than for one jot of God's Word to fall to the ground. Jesus once told the Jewish leaders of His day: *"For truly I say to you, until heaven and earth pass away, not the smallest letter or stroke shall pass from the Law until all is accomplished"* (Matthew 5:18). Through the prophet Isaiah, the Lord says: *"The grass withers, the flower fades, but the word of our God stands forever"* (Isaiah 40:8).

Walk on, through and around . . .

God has already made ample provision not only for you to accomplish His purpose, but also for you to possess the inheritance He has destined for you. However, your human condition—sin and its fallouts—always stands in the way of your purpose. Quite often God may have to call you to your wildernesses to prepare you for crossing over your Jordan, en route to your destiny. You must also be aware that your provision and godly inheritance may be in the possession of someone else; but those facts do not really matter.

> **There is no possession without confession, and no inheritance without walking the distance.**

The children of Israel lived on land for which they had not labored; inherited cities which they did not build; ate from vineyards which they did not plant; and so can you. If you are standing on the banks of your Jordan, it is time for you to get ready for your next move. Dispossession is about to take place. God is ready and able to dispossess the enemy of all that he has stolen from you, and give to you the inheritance He has ordained for you.

However, before you are able to possess and inherit, you must be prepared to confess and walk on your territory. There is no possession without confession, and no inheritance without walking the distance. The word "confession" comes from the compound Greek word *homologeō—homo*, which means *same* or *like*; and *logos*, which means *word* or *speech*. When put together, the compound word means to say the same thing; to agree with or confirm what someone else says.

Consequently, when we confess with our mouth the promises which God has spoken in His Word, we place ourselves in agreement with Him, and in a position to receive exactly what His Word says. Confession of faith calls the things which are not (visible, nonetheless real) as though they were (Romans 4:17). It literally brings into existence the promises spoken and confirmed by the unfailing Word of God. Joshua repeatedly rehearsed in the ears of the children of Israel all God had promised their forefathers, accomplished through Moses, and promised to do through his (Joshua) leadership.

Confession must also be followed by positive action. You must not only talk the talk, but also walk the talk. Be prepared to walk on, through and around your territory—land, home, property, vehicle, etc. If the territory is immaterial, or of such that you cannot walk on, through or around it, then do what Joshua told the three-party scouts of the seven tribes—that is, write a careful description of all that you see or imagine (Joshua 18:4), and take it to God in prayer and confession.

Think big! Remember, the earth and its fullness belongs to your God (Psalm 24:1). Therefore you walk; you own. Failure to walk means failure to possess and inherit.

Your Life-time Warranty

. . . I will never leave thee, nor forsake thee.

Hebrews 13:5

God had promised Joshua that no one would be able to stand before him all the days of his life, because His abiding presence would never fail or forsake him. This divine pledge holds true for everyone who puts his trust in the Almighty, for His Word guarantees that *those who hopefully wait for Him will not be put to shame* (Isaiah 49:23). It was the presence of God and Joshua's obedience to all His commands that made this leader of Israel an invincible power in the earth. His powerful, positive leadership won the people's confidence and placed them in a position to be the beneficiaries of all that God promised him. Israel obeyed because Joshua obeyed and insisted on their compliance to the will of Jehovah. This made all the difference in the outcome of Israel's future.

Your life-time warranty on all God's promises concerning your future destiny is under-written in the blood of Jesus, but its full benefits are hinged on your unswerving obedience to all its conditions. Although your heavenly Father pledges never to leave or forsake you, and guarantees your victory over every opponent and obstacle in the path to your destiny, He can only do so as you co-operate with all that He requires of you.

> **Your destiny is already secured in Christ ...
> get ready to walk!**

Consequently, knowing and following all His instructions for your life is of critical importance to the type of advancement you will make in your pursuit of your life's purpose. In view of this truth, you become your greatest enemy between you and your destiny. Your attitude towards God and His revealed will — not the situation or behavior of others — is the ONLY factor that will determine whether you become a success or a failure.

Your destiny is already secured in Christ. No man,

human system or organization can change it, or prevent you from achieving it. Just as the political and military establishments of the many nations which occupied Canaan's territories could not stand before Joshua and his civilian hosts, so no one, and nothing, would be able to stand before you all the days of your life. You do not have to fight any wars. God promises to do all the fighting for you if you will only allow Him. He says that your enemies will come at you in one way, but will flee before you in seven ways (Deuteronomy 28:7).

The Almighty God is not only your life-time Counselor and Guide. He is also your invincible Champion. Trust Him! As the God of history, He has an unblemished track record of unprecedented victories over all His opponents and all the obstacles they placed before His children. A favorite author of mine once said: "We have nothing to fear for the future, except as we shall forget the way the Lord has led us, and His teaching in our past history."[1] Nothing can be more ingenuous than this truth.

Israel's journey from the clay pits of Egypt to the beautiful cities and fruitful vineyards of their promised homeland bears clear, countless testimonies of God's mighty acts on behalf of His covenant children. What else is left for me to say to you, dear reader, than to ask the poignant question: How long will you put off entering in to take possession of what God has already given to you? Examine your platform, stand on His promises, and get ready to walk!

Standing on the Promises[2]

Standing on the promises of Christ my King,
Through eternal ages let His praises ring;
Glory in the highest I will shout and sing,
Standing on the promises of God.

Standing on the promises that cannot fail,
When the howling storms of doubt and fear assail,
By the living Word of God I shall prevail,
Standing on the promises of God.

Standing on the promises of Christ the Lord,
Bound to Him eternally by love's strong chord,
Overcoming daily with the Spirit's sword,
Standing on the promises of God.

Refrain

Standing, standing,
Standing on the promises of Christ my Savior;
Standing, standing,
I'm standing on the promises of God.

Notes:

1. Ellen G. White, *Testimonies for the Church, vol. 9* (Idaho: Pacific Press Publishing Association, 1948), 10.
2. Hymn written by R. Kelso Carter, quoted in Seventh-day Adventist Church Hymnal (Hagerstown, MD: Review and Herald Publishing Association, 1988).

CHAPTER 3

Eliminate Your Fears: Embrace God's Endorsement

"Be strong and of a good courage . . . Only be thou strong and very courageous; . . . Have I not commanded thee? Be strong and of a good courage; be not afraid, neither be thou dismayed: for the Lord thy God is with thee whithersoever thou goest."

Joshua 1:6, 7, 9, KJV

*W*hen God appeared to Moses and Joshua in the pillar of cloud which stood at the entrance of the tent of meeting, *He commissioned Joshua the son of Nun, and said, "Be strong and courageous, for you shall bring the sons of Israel into the land which I swore to them, and I will be with you"* (Deuteronomy 31:23).

It would appear that the words and tone of this commission were quite necessary and obviously very important, requiring God to repeat them three more times after they were first announced to the new appointee. Why would God repeat Himself in such a manner, and, in the last case, with the authoritative question? *Have I not commanded thee? Be strong and of a good courage. . .* (Joshua 1:9). Although the reasons were never clearly stated in the historical account of Israel's journey, they were partially alluded to in God's statement to Moses immediately before He commissioned Joshua.

> [16]*The LORD said to Moses, "Behold, you are about to lie down with your fathers; and this people will arise and play the harlot with the strange gods of the land, into the midst of which they are going, and will forsake Me and break My covenant which I have made with them. . .* [20]*For when I bring them into the land flowing with milk and honey, which I swore to their fathers, and they have eaten and are satisfied and become prosperous, then they will turn to other gods and serve them, and spurn Me and break My covenant."*

> Deuteronomy 31:16, 20

God was quite familiar with the rotten reputation of the people He delivered from the clay pits of Egypt; protected from enemies and the elements of the wilderness; and provided for and preserved through forty years of wilderness wandering. He witnessed firsthand, Moses' wearisome toiling with their barefaced ingratitude to his patient caring leadership; how they provoked him to anger and finally pushed him over the edge at Kadesh Barnea. There, instead of doing as God commanded him—that is, to speak to the rock—he struck the rock twice. Because of this major slip-up, he was permitted only to see the Promised Land, but was debarred from entering the same. These heartless rebels were able to bring out the worst in the best of leaders, and cause him to lose the opportunity of his life-time—the satisfying joy of entering Canaan with them, and of witnessing their settlement in the land of promise.

God knew precisely what Israel was capable of doing and was surely preparing Joshua for the challenge. Although Joshua was an eyewitness of Israel's rebellious conduct, and also an unfortunate victim of the same, he was not their leader, and therefore was not accountable to God for their behavior as Moses was. It is one thing to walk as a protégé of a leader then, and but something altogether different to actually walk in that leader's shoes. Now the buck was going to stop at Joshua and he had to show himself "man" enough for the job.

Another possible reason for God's caution to Joshua was His knowledge of the heathen nations who occupied the various cities and territories of the land of Canaan. These people were trained in the art of war and were not prepared to merely sit back and watch a pack of ex-slaves move in and dispossess them of all they had worked so hard to provide for themselves and their future generations. Israel's fear of the descendants of Anak was another major hurdle in the path of their advancement through the Promise Land. It would take uncommon courage on the part of Joshua to mobilize and motivate his inexperienced, undisciplined hosts to go up against the "giants" whose name once struck terror and rebellion throughout the entire camp of Israel. Let us look at the report the ten spies gave to Moses and review the reaction of the people:

> [27]*Thus they told him, and said, "We went in to the land where you sent us; and it certainly does flow with milk and honey, and this is its fruit.* [28]*Nevertheless, the people who live in the land are strong, and the cities are fortified and very large; and moreover, we saw the descendants of Anak there.* [29]*Amalek is living in the land of the Negev and the Hittites and the Jebusites and the Amorites are living in the hill country, and the Canaanites are living by the sea and by the side of the Jordan. . .* [33]*There also we saw the Nephilim (the sons of Anak are part of the Nephilim); and we became like grasshoppers in our own sight, and so we were in their sight."*

> NU 14:1*Then all the congregation lifted up their voices and cried, and the people wept that night.* [2]*All the*

*sons of Israel grumbled against Moses and Aaron;
and the whole congregation said to them, "Would that
we had died in the land of Egypt! Or would that we
had died in this wilderness! ³Why is the LORD
bringing us into this land, to fall by the sword? Our
wives and our little ones will become plunder; would
it not be better for us to return to Egypt?" ⁴So they
said to one another, "Let us appoint a leader and
return to Egypt."*

Numbers 13:27-33; 14:1-4

Indeed, Israel, a very unruly multitude, was
conditioned to respond only to the cracking of the slave-
master's whip as it made contact with their aching, overloaded
backs. No doubt, Joshua had his work set aside for him, and
the merciful God of his fathers was challenging him to be
prepared mentally and emotionally to take on the job.

The Power of Affirmation

Be strong and of a good courage . . .

The words of the above text were not intended to be
a request, or to be regarded as a suggestion. They are very
short, positive and decisive, and were given as a command.

Be strong!

In this command, the word "you" is understood, and the verb "be" implies an inherent quality in the one that is called to be—that is, in this case, Joshua. Joshua is called to be strong because he has the capacity to be strong. However, there is much more going on here than meets the eye. Strong refers to more than just physical strength. It also connotes spiritual and moral firmness, not easily persuaded to change a course of action. Some people demonstrate strength only when they are running with the crowd, or flowing with the tide of "positive" events occurring in their lives. Yet, when the odds are against them, or they have to stand alone, the quality of their strength appears very hollow and weak.

Although Joshua had proven himself very strong and unyielding in the face of great opposition, taking charge of the unruly multitude and leading them successfully over the Jordan and into the land of promise required much more. Consequently, God's command for him to be strong could not rest on his past accomplishments or on his frail humanity, but only on the strength and power of the Almighty flowing through him. Joshua is commanded to be strong because the God watching over him is strong. This was a command for him to lean on the unfailing arm of Jehovah.

In his final prophecy regarding the future of his son, Joseph, dying Jacob declared that "*his [Joseph's] bow abode* *in strength, and the arms of his hands were made <u>strong by the hands of the mighty God of Jacob</u>"* (Genesis 49:24). Isaiah, the prophet, described God as great in might and strong in power (Isaiah 40:26). He is the One who makes His people strong.

Be Courageous!

This command is just as forceful as the first. In fact, they come together— *[you], be strong and [you], be of a good courage.* While strength points more to spiritual and mental steadiness, courage speaks to bold, fearless, staying power that provides mental, emotional and moral toughness in the face of danger, opposition and hardship. Joshua needed both strength and *good* courage not just for dealing with the unpredictable behavior of his rowdy people, but, even more so, for the challenge of leading them against the well-trained military machinery of the nations who occupied the settlements in Canaan.

Good courage can only come from God.

However, Joshua found his source of courage in the strength and faithfulness of the Almighty God of his forefathers. That courage was good because its foundation was God and not Joshua. Courage based on one's own strength and ability may be able to sustain a person in certain situations, but *good* courage can only come from God. Apart from the *good* courage facilitated by the Almighty, Israel's attempt to dispossess and occupy the territories of Canaan would have been a suicide mission of catastrophic proportions. As history records, Joshua's strength and *good* courage became the touchstone for Israel's confidence in responding positively to his commands, and in following his leadership across the Jordan into the land of their inheritance.

When God is in Your Picture

We have come to times in the history of our world when there is the prevailing need for uncommon strength and courage. Chaos and uncertainty exist all around us. Fear, anxiety, distress, emotional upheaval and depression abound on every hand. The unexpected, precipitous collapse of global economies and the growing threat of environmental annihilation keep the masses in a state of constant panic and restlessness.

In fact, the time of the end, which Jesus predicted would suddenly come upon the inhabitants of the earth, seems very imminent. This time, He said, would be characterized by wars and rumors of wars, pestilences, earthquakes in many places, very turbulent weather patterns, and increasing heart attacks due to fear and anxiety—all of which we are experiencing right now.

> *[10]Then said he unto them, nation shall rise against nation, and kingdom against kingdom: [11]And great earthquakes shall be in divers places, and famines, and pestilences; and fearful sights and great signs shall there be from heaven . . . [25]And there shall be signs in the sun, and in the moon, and in the stars; and upon the earth distress of nations, with perplexity; the sea and the waves roaring; [26]Men's hearts failing them for fear, and for looking after those things which are coming on the earth: for the powers of heaven shall be shaken.*

Luke 21:10, 11, 25, 26

Obviously, this is not a very pretty picture, and in the midst of this threatening, fearsome jungle, your mighty Jordan flows. Reader, you and I both know that we need the God of Joshua right now—like yesterday. The truth is that God is always ready, even before we sense our need of Him. His words of encouragement and endorsement to Joshua are just as authentic and good for you and me: *"Have I not commanded thee? Be strong and of a good courage; be not afraid, neither be thou dismayed: for the Lord thy God is with thee whithersoever thou goest*" (Joshua 1:9, KJV).

God's got your back!

God's command is always supported by His presence and faithfulness. It really does not matter what the size or condition of your Jordan situation is, what enemies lie between you and your God-appointed destiny, or who is currently in possession of your future inheritance. Those facts do not really matter when God's got your back and is leading your charge. Therefore, *be strong and courageous*, because you have more going for you than what is coming out against you. Listen what your almighty Commander says to you:

> [25]*Do not be afraid of sudden fear nor of the onslaught of the wicked when it comes;* [26]*For <u>the LORD will be your confidence</u> and <u>will keep your foot from being caught</u>.*

> Proverb 3:25, 26

Here is something you must never forget, even though it is something that most people misunderstand. While the situations of your life may bring many challenges to you, your success in negotiating your way through them is never really about you. Rather, it is always about the grace of God facilitating and empowering you; nothing else. God had to teach His servant Moses this precious lesson in a very humbling, heart-wrenching way.

When ungrateful Israel grumbled for water in the wilderness of Zin, God told Moses: *"take the rod; and you and your brother Aaron assemble the congregation and <u>speak to the rock</u> before their eyes, that it may yield its water. You shall thus bring forth water for them out of the rock and let the congregation and their beasts drink"* (Numbers 20:8).

However, instead of following through with God's command, Moses did not only make the fatal decision to strike the rock, but also insinuated in his outburst that he and his brother Aaron (not God) were the ones providing the congregation with drinking water. God's immediate judgment pronounced upon His faithful servant is a very serious and timely warning to all, especially those whom He places in authority over His people.

[9]So Moses took the rod from before the LORD, just as He had commanded him; [10]and Moses and Aaron gathered the assembly before the rock. And he said to them, "Listen now, you rebels; shall we bring forth water for you out of this rock?" [11]Then Moses lifted up his hand and struck the rock twice with his rod; and water came forth abundantly, and the

congregation and their beasts drank. ¹²But the LORD said to Moses and Aaron, "Because you have not believed Me, to treat Me as holy in the sight of the sons of Israel, <u>therefore you shall not bring this assembly into the land which I have given them</u>."

Numbers 20:9-12, KJV

Joshua learned a very important lesson that day. He was most present when God set aside his revered predecessor (Moses) and his brother (Aaron), forfeiting their most treasured desire and privilege of leading the nation of Israel into the land of promise. Later, God would choose him to complete what Moses was denied because of his sin in a most pivotal moment of his life. Our triumph over life's vicissitudes is never really about us, and what we "think" we are bringing to the table in terms of "our" skills and abilities. Rather, it is always about God accommodating and blessing us—nothing else.

The secret about successfully dealing with your Jordan and attaining your abundance, is having the Almighty God as the source of your confidence. This is the one sure way of keeping your feet from being caught in the snares and pitfalls of your enemies. God already knows all the plans of your enemies and will either show you how to avert them or find a way around, through or over them. He also knows how to make your enemies show favor to you, even when they have no intention of doing so (Proverb 16:7).

The Bible also says that the king's heart (and certainly your enemies) is like channels of water in the hands of the Lord, and He can turn it any way He wishes (Proverbs 21:1). Even if your boss is obnoxious or oppressive, or the owner of the property does not like you, his/her heart is in the hand of the Lord and He knows how to turn it in your favor. *Be strong and very courageous!*

King David was a man with life's situations similar to, and in most cases even worse than, those of the average human being. He faced many obstacles and near-death experiences on his way from an obscure sheepfold in the Judean hills to the favored throne of Israel; from being an insignificant shepherd-boy to becoming the most notable king in Jewish history, and the forefather of our Lord, Jesus Christ.

"And behold, you will conceive in your womb and bear a son, and you shall name Him Jesus. [32]He will be great and will be called the Son of the Most High; and the Lord God will give Him the throne of His father David; [33]and He will reign over the house of Jacob forever, and His kingdom will have no end."

Luke 1:31-33

What an amazing legacy! Then again, nothing is too hard for the God of all the earth. Although it was not always easy sailing for David, God always had his back. On many occasions, while his enemies were plotting his death, God was already establishing ways of escape for His favored servant. In his favorite memoirs, David left us this prized note that ends with the rhetorical question: *The LORD is on my side; I will not fear: what can man do unto me?* (Psalm 118:6). Absolutely nothing! God is our sun and shield (Psalm 84:11) and the precious Rock of our salvation (2 Samuel 22:47). My beloved reader, whatever the condition of the mighty Jordan that is before you, *be strong and very courageous*, for God Almighty's got your back!

Facing Down Your Fears

"for God did not give us a spirit of cowardice, but rather a spirit of power and of love and of self-discipline."

2 Timothy 1:7, NRSV

Fear is the product of our logical assessment of our human condition and situation. It is the result of our bringing our reasoning to bear on our perception of a reality that appears to threaten our sense of safety and well-being.

Someone insightfully described fear as *f*alse *e*xperiences *a*ppearing *r*eal — using the letters in the word (FEAR) as an acronym. Nonetheless, the very interesting thing about fear is that it did not originate from God. It became an integral part of the human condition at the time of the Fall.[1] Satan planted in Adam and Eve the seed of doubt that yielded the deceitful, corrupt fruit, which instinctively gave human intelligence pre-eminence over the infallible Word of the Creator.

The diabolical implant of this satanic glitch within the psyche of all Adam's descendants, created the operational malfunction which automatically turned the soul to self in place of God, and to human reason instead of faith in the Almighty. Consequently, whenever choices were to be made, God was either a non-entity or simply an afterthought when all other considerations had failed. Self and human intellect, not God, became the autopilot of every human being.

> **Through the "Fall," self and human reason became the auto-pilot of the human soul.**

Thus, Satan paved the way to make us prisoners of fear by locking us up in the logic box of our minds. Even though God has made ample provisions for us to be free, by default, we continue to turn to self and other imprisoned humans, instead of the Almighty, for help with our problems.

RUTHVEN J. ROY

The devil deceived Eve into trusting her "better judgment" over the expressed will of her Maker. She then became the medium of seduction to her husband who placed his love for her (another product of human reason/knowledge) above God's direct command to him: *"from any tree of the garden you may eat freely; but from the tree of the knowledge of good and evil you shall not eat, for in the day that you eat from it you will surely die"* (Genesis 2:16, 17).[2]

Immediately following Adam's sin, the disgraced pair was suddenly overcome by fear and dread as their thoughts of God were instantly changed by the reality of their transgression. Therefore, when God arrived on the scene for His usual fellowship with His children, Adam and Eve resorted to "hiding" themselves from His presence. As soon as God called out for Adam, he uttered the unalterable truth. *He said, "I heard the sound of You in the garden, and I WAS AFRAID because I was naked; so I hid myself"* (Genesis 3:10).

As descendants of Adam, we are prone to be overcome by fear, because the satanic glitch made self and human reason the auto-pilot of our souls. The devil tricked our fore-parents into a perfect Catch 22, and we became the collateral victims of the satanic plot. As a direct result of the "Fall," the human mind has been wired to try involuntarily, to solve its own problems and life's issues, making it appear very natural for us to automatically query things occurring in

, we search for the logical answers to those he why, when, how and so forth. However, when the prince of the power of the air,[3] the chief engineer of our mental malfunction,[4] creates mind-boggling disturbances in our environment—for example, "sudden" illness, death, economic hardship, social chaos, etc.—, incalculable, unwarranted pressure is exerted on our system of logic. The baleful result from all the disordered confusion is cycles of fear, panic, worry, depression, insanity, severe illness and even death.

> **God provides the strength to "be strong" and the power to be mighty.**

In spite of all this, God's good news says that fear does not have to be your master, and you do not have to be a helpless captive of the enemy either. Your heavenly Father has made available to you the power to confront and vanquish your fears, and to released you completely from the devil's grip. You may be in the middle of a nightmare or some terrible, fearful dilemma, but what you are experiencing is not the complete truth about your real situation.

Do not despair; "b*e strong and of a good courage; be not afraid, neither be thou dismayed, for the Lord thy God is with you whithersoever thou goest*" (Joshua 1:9). I can imagine some of you saying right now: "Well, that's easy to say, but I am in the middle of a hell right now, and being strong and courageous is not what I am feeling." "I am frustrated and scared, that's what!" I can hear others of you saying: "I want to be strong and courageous, but I really don't know how."

Here is my very candid answer to you. You need to change your focus and rewire the logic switch of your mind. Yes, you read me right. Turn your focus away from you and your seemingly insurmountable situation and focus on God Almighty, the Creator of heaven and earth, who can change your situation forever by one word from His lips. You see the strength to "be strong" does not and cannot come from you. When you are dealing with an adversary as the devil and all the evil and troubles he brings into your life, your humanity would never suffice.

The strength to "be strong" comes only from one source—God. The Bible admonishes you to *"be strong in the Lord and the power of His might"* (Ephesians 6:10). Notice that the strength is the Lord, and the power comes from His might. This is why you must change your focus and think and turn your full attention on God and His limitless power and inexhaustible solution options.

Remember that it was the wrong focus that got humanity into mess we encounter daily in the first place. Satan deceived Eve into turning her attention away from God and His Word to herself and her thoughts. As long as you keep your focus on your Jordan situation, you will be overcome by fear. I invite you to turn your attention to your Father, for He is saying to you:

> *"Do not tremble and do not be afraid; have I not long since announced it to you and declared it? And you are My witnesses. Is there any God besides Me, or is there any other Rock? I know of none."*

Isaiah 44:8

> *"Do not fear, for I am with you; do not anxiously look about you, for I am your God. I will strengthen you, surely I will help you, Surely I will uphold you with My righteous right hand."*

Isaiah 41:10

Stop anxiously looking about you, for God saw your situation before it even came to you. It just may be that He has allowed it so that He could get your attention. Weigh in on God's perspective. Your Jordan is not meant to drown you, but to deliver you from drowning in your own devices. As your Jordan swells, correspondingly, your anxiety level rises. Your anxiety level is connected to your continuous focus on what is happening in and around you, and your logical

79

assessment of the same. If this is where you are right now, make the deliberated decision to change your focus immediately! Train your thoughts on God, who is enthroned above your situation.

Flick your mental switch from logic to faith and hold.

I know that this is not very easy to do, because it is not an automatic response of the human psyche. However, you must deliberately force yourself to do this, beginning right now. Detach yourself for a moment several times each day to focus on God and His Word. Then try to increase the time you spend with the Almighty no matter what comes up. Perform this simple exercise every day and you will begin to experience the most amazing results.

Hebrews 11:3 says that by faith the worlds were framed by the Word of God, who made everything from absolutely nothing. You can use the same word of God to reframe your chaotic world into a haven of peace and rest for your soul. Start right now, and even if it does not turn out perfect immediately, keep on trying. Remember, you are not looking for perfection here. Your main goal is renewal— spirit, soul and body.

You are re-establishing a direct link to your Creator. Humanity lost it after the "Fall." New pathways must be developed in your psyche that would make you amenable to depending on God more and upon yourself less. This is the very opposite to what the devil has placed in you through the disgrace of Adam your forefather. More will be said about this in the chapters that follow.

Now, you cannot stop at just changing your focus; you must go one step further, while you are so inclined. Switch from your logic and self-dependence to faith and surrender to God Almighty. Switch from sizing up your situation by your estimate of your inadequate human potential to the surrendering of everything to the care of the God who knows no failure. When you do, and patiently WAIT on Him, He will most certainly show up. He is not only your *refuge and strength*, but also, and always, your *very present help* in the time of trouble (Psalm 46:1). He says in the above scripture that He will strengthen you, help you, and surely uphold you with His righteous right hand (Isaiah 41:10).

Your trouble may be that you do not like the word WAIT, and you are usually playing switch-a-rue with your focus — steering at your situation, while only momentarily glancing at God. You, like many others, may be affected by an acute case of Attention Deficit Hyperactivity Disorder (or ADHD) when you have to wait on God. However, you must flick your mental switch from logic to faith and hold that position. God will come through.

You must learn to be still before the Majesty of the universe. He says that whenever you assume that posture, He will let you know that He is indeed God—that is, the real Boss over all your situations—and that He (not you) will be exalted in the earth (Psalm 46:10). Moreover, He promises that only those who wait on Him will have their strength renewed, and will be empowered to rise over their earthly circumstances like soaring eagles under the lift of a steady stream of wind (Isaiah 40:31).

Therefore, you must endeavor to keep your focus on God and give all your momentary light afflictions (2 Corinthians 4:17) and concerns over to Him. As a matter of fact, the Scriptures say that although those light afflictions are real, they are always producing something far more wonderful for you in the *causal* (spiritual) realm that is yet to manifest. Take a good look at that text again:

For our light and momentary troubles are achieving for us an eternal glory that far outweighs them all. [18]So we fix our eyes not on what is seen, but on what is unseen. For what is seen is temporary, but what is unseen is eternal.

2 Corinthians 4:17, 18, NIV

Your difficulty arises whenever you focus your

attention on your momentary troubles (*what is seen*) instead of on God (*the unseen*), who is always working out everything for your good (Romans 8:28), because He cares for you (1 Peter 5:7). Incidentally, Jesus asked the most practical question for your logical mind: "*And who of you by being worried can add a single hour to his life?* (Matthew 6:27).

The sad truth is that you do the same worrying every day of your life and you can't seem to figure out that that has not added one iota to any solution to your problems in the past. You have become the victims of your own minds, trapped helplessly in the revolving cycle of your own thoughts—locked in the puny space of your logic boxes.

Your heavenly Father wants to set you free from this deadly debacle. He promises to sustain you in perfect peace if you could only keep your mind focused on Him (Isaiah 26:3). Paul says that when you do this, *the peace of God, which surpasses all comprehension, will guard your hearts and your minds in Christ Jesus* (Philippians 4:7). Remember this, dear reader: Fear and dread are the direct product of human reason, and these only lead to frustration, fatigue, depression and death.

Peace and confidence are the direct result of faith and surrender to the unfailing care of a loving God, and will lead you to satisfaction, vigor, optimism and abundant life. The enemy of your soul uses perplexing distractions in your external environment to engage your senses and keep your mind in perpetual chaos and confusion. Thus, he entices you to shift focus from God and His will for your life. God, on the other hand, uses His peace in your soul, made possible through your faithful dependence on Him, to override and defy whatever is occurring in your surroundings.

Agree With God

The thief comes only to steal and kill and destroy; I came that they may have life, and have it abundantly.

John 10:10

God has made ample provision for you to achieve your purpose in life, but the evil one will do anything, will use anyone and any situation to try to rob you of your inheritance. You must be determined not to allow this to happen to you. How do you accomplish this? Link with your Savior and "tag-team" your enemy. The Bible says that the reason Christ came into the world was to destroy the works of the devil (1 John 3:8).

There is absolutely no need for you to face your Jordan alone when your Savior is willing, able and ready to help you cross over. As you focus your attention upon Him, learn how to say what He says and not what you think. Please do not miss this, because it is a very important kingdom principle that will yield stupendous results.

If Adam and Eve had simply said to the devil what the Creator had commanded them, and stuck to that, we would not be in such a messed up world like ours is today. Mankind was designed to live forever by every word that proceeded from the mouth of the living God. This is exactly what Jesus did when He was severely tested by the devil in the wilderness of temptation. He simply stuck to what was written in the Word of God—*it is written* (Matthew 4:1-10).

Spend more time trusting than thinking.

As long as the enemy can get you off message to say what you think instead of what God has designed for your safety in His Word, he will certainly gain control over your mind. This is the simple reason why intelligent people have a very difficult time coming to faith and peace in Jesus Christ. The enemy deceives them into thinking that they are very smart, and that they could figure everything out on their own. He still whispers to them: *you could be like God, knowing good and evil* (Genesis 3:5).

Do not buy into all the fanciful philosophies of men and this world. The entire planet is already messed up from all that human wisdom has to offer. The Bible says that the wisdom of this world is foolish (1 Corinthians 3:19), natural and demonic, leading to jealousy, selfish ambition, disorder and every evil thing (James 3:15, 16).

With all our head knowledge and earthly wisdom we have created all types of disasters in our lives, and are desperately seeking for ways out of our nerve-grinding troubles. No doubt, your sense of failure and frustration may have dampened your spirit, leaving you dwindling hopes regarding your dreams for your future life. God's command to Joshua comes with a new spirit of urgency to you.

"Have not I commanded thee? Be strong and of a good courage; be not afraid, neither be thou dismayed: for the LORD thy God is with thee whithersoever thou goest."

Joshua 1:9, KJV

Cease your futile, restless strivings. Focus on your God, and yield your wandering mind to the authority of His unchanging Word. Align your tongue in agreement with Its precepts and let your ears hear you affirming God's command: *I am strong and very courageous, for the Lord my God is with me wherever I go.* You are strong because the God who commands you is strong. You are courageous because the God who is empowering you cannot be intimidated by any human situation.

Your strength and courage are not based on how you see or feel about yourself—that has nothing to with anything, but fear. Your focus and dependence is upon God who is able to do all things well. David said the Lord was the strength of his life and he had absolutely no reason to fear anyone (Psalm 27:1). Your strength and power is not in yourself and your abilities, but in God almighty.

Are you still trying to be the strength of your life? Where has that gotten you in the past? The undeniable truth is that you are on the other side of numberless situations in your life—some of which you even thought would have destroyed you, and possible others very close to you—and you do not even know how you ever got to this present point. But you are here! What have you really contributed, short of worrying yourself sick and messing things up, to bringing yourself out whole from all the major adversities that have flowed through your life?

Nevertheless, you continue to put yourselves through the same sordid grind, twisting and turning in the constricted logic box of your mind, as you face your current Jordan nightmares. How did you ever come through all your adversities that are presently behind you? Deep inside of you, you know it was not on account of anything that you personally did; but chances are you may be thinking, "it just happened."

Well, nothing just happens! My family mechanic, who does not hold any particular religious beliefs, has a very peculiar confidence that he expresses in the face of current crisis situation in his life. He always say to me, "I have been around the block long enough to know that everything works itself out. It usually does." Thus, he keeps right on doing what seems necessary for him and leaves the rest to work itself out. What my mechanic friend does not realize just yet, is that his "peculiar" confidence activates the very powerful hand of the unseen God of the universe, who allows His copious streams of mercy to flow upon the just and the unjust in this world.

Nothing just happens!!!

God has already been working in your favor amid all the challenges of your life, whether you realize that or not. How much more would He allow you to accomplish if you were to agree with all He says to you, and about you, in His Word. There is no need for you to continue to operate in the crammed space of your overcrowded mind to only escalate your troubles. This is your time to let go and let God man the controls of your life.

Commit yourself and all your affairs to Him. Do not allow yourself to be frustrated and shackled by the mere facts of your current position any longer. Release yourself forever from these chains by daily embracing the timeless truth that God is already working through, and working out everything in the lives of all those who love and trust Him.

And we know that God causes <u>all things</u> to work together for good to those who love God, to those who are called according to His purpose.

Romans 8:28

Remember, it is only the truth—not the facts—that will make you free. If you keep your focus on the facts of you situation, you will be imprisoned by them. However, there is absolutely no factual prison in your fleeting earthly existence from which the Truth[5] cannot break you free. Therefore, *be strong and of a good courage . . . for the Lord thy God is with thee whithersoever thou goest* (Joshua 1:9).

Divine Recall

Have you ever driven a vehicle that had to be recalled by the manufacturers because of some glitch in one or more of its operating systems that rendered that vehicle potentially unsafe for use? Well, I have. I owned a Chrysler Jeep that once had to be recalled because of some inherent weakness in the braking system. The truth is that I had problems every

89

winter with that vehicle because the brakes would not hold regardless of the speed I was travelling, and what adjustment my mechanic made to it.

I did not know that the vehicle had a manufacturing flaw that would make it a would-be threat to my family and me. When I receive the letter from Chrysler Corporation saying that my vehicle had been recalled because of a glitch in the brake system, boy did I feel a sense of relief? I promptly took the vehicle in to a designated dealership and had the brake assembly completely checked and parts replaced free of charge.

I have heard of other frustrating, harrowing motor-vehicle stories that have aided my understanding of what the devil has done to the operating system of the human mind. My braking problem was quite straightforward and very easy to address, but when a computer chip or wiring harness of a vehicle has a manufacturing flaw, the headaches are endless. Consider therefore, the perpetual cycles of headaches, frustration, fear, anxiety, distress, depression, sickness and even death that have beset the human family because of the seed of self-centeredness the enemy had planted in the psyche of our fore-parents, Adam and Eve.

God has a replacement for His divine recall—JESUS.

This self-centered disposition has made mankind the helpless victim of his very deceitful and wicked mind. Jeremiah, the prophet of the Lord, uttered these truths in the following way:

The heart is deceitful above all things, and desperately wicked: who can know it?

Jeremiah 17:9

I know, O LORD, that a man's way is not in himself, Nor is it in a man who walks to direct his steps. [24]Correct me, O LORD, but with justice; Not with Your anger, or You will bring me to nothing.

Jeremiah 10:23, 24

The voice of wisdom also declared, *there is a way which seems right to a man, but its end is the way of death* (Proverbs 16:25). However, no one explained more clearly than Paul the continuous frustration we have dealing with the fallout of the genetic flaw of our fallen human nature. He complained:
[14]*For we know that the law is spiritual; but I am of the flesh, sold into slavery under sin. [15]I do not understand my own actions. For I do not do what I want, but I do the very thing I hate. . . [19]For I do not do the good I want, but the evil I do not want is what*

I do. [20] Now if I do what I do not want, it is no longer I that do it, but sin that dwells within me. [21] So I find it to be a law that when I want to do what is good, evil lies close at hand. [22] For I delight in the law of God in my inmost self, [23] but I see in my members another law at war with the law of my mind, making me captive to the law of sin that dwells in my members.

Romans 7:15-23, NRSV

In sheer frustration, the apostle cried out in the very next verse (v. 24), *"wretched man that I am! Who will rescue me from this body of death?"* But then He remembered the divine recall of the first Adam man and his new flawless replacement, Jesus Christ, and he shouted for joy in verse 25, *"thanks be to God through Jesus Christ our Lord!"*

Friend of mind, you do not have to continue playing your life like a defective record that gets stuck every time in the middle of your tune. You do not have to remain stuck in the cycle of your frustration and fear for the rest of your life. *Be strong and of a good courage*, for God has a replacement for your divine recall, Jesus. His Word says that He was manifested (or came) to break the power of the devil's glitch in your soul (1 John 3:8). Why not exchange your life with all its headaches and heartaches for the life of God's new flawless replacement, Jesus Christ. Receive Him into your life today; I mean, even right now.

Now, here is a prayer to help you do just that. **Loving Jesus, thank you for being the perfect replacement for my troubled life, and for dying in my place on the cross of Calvary for all my sins. I completely release myself and all my concerns to your divine care, and receive Your life into my heart right now. I accept You as my Savior and Lord. I am sorry for all of my sins, for all of the times I have turned away from You. Cleanse me in Your precious blood and help me to live a life of obedience to Your perfect will. Teach me how to agree with You in the confession of Your Holy Word, and fill me with Your peace, Your strength and Your courage to face each and every day, I pray in Your holy name, Amen.**

What A Friend We Have in Jesus
What a Friend we have in Jesus
All our sins and grief to bear
What a privilege to carry
Everything to God in prayer.
O what peace we often forfeit
O what needless pain we bear
All because we do not carry
Everything to God in prayer[6]

Notes:

1. The "Fall" refers to the moral disgrace of Adam and Eve in the Garden of Eden when they disobeyed their Creator, allowing sin to become a permanent curse on the human race.

2. For a fuller understand of this very important glitch in the human psyche, please read chapters 1 and 4 of my provocative volume, *The Imitation of God: the Amazing Secret of Living His Life* (Berrien Springs, MI: Rehoboth Publishing, 2010).

3. Prince of the power of the air is another alias for the devil. See Ephesians 2:2.

4. Mental malfunction is the deadly effect of the satanic glitch in the human psyche that causes an individual to instinctively and continuously turn to himself, not God, for guidance and answers to all of life's issues.

5. Truth here refers to Jesus, the Son of man, and His word – John 14:6; 8:31, 32, 36.

6. First verse of the hymn, *What a Friend We Have in Jesus*, by John M. Scriven, 1855.

CHAPTER 4

Position Yourself:
Make The Commitment To Obey

"Only be strong and very courageous; be careful to do according to all the law which Moses My servant commanded you; <u>do not turn from it to the right or to the left</u>, so that you may have success wherever you go."

Joshua 1:7

*G*od's instructions to His servant Joshua were very clear and unambiguous. He had no intention to reinvent the wheel with this new appointment to leadership. He was not going to set up a fresh set of requirements for Joshua. For Him, a change in leadership did not represent a change in policy and procedures. His expectations are always firm, just as all His promises are sure. God meant to keep all the pledges of the covenant He made with His friend Abraham, but he was not going to excuse any of the patriarch's descendants for their disobedience to the terms written therein.

Therefore, God's command to Joshua, *"be strong and very courageous,"* was meant to bolster his confidence in his newly assigned position, and to strengthen his resolve against the warring nations in the land Canaan. These were mere spin-offs of a much larger issue, and God already knew what He was going to do about them. Of greater value to God was the moral strength and courage of Israel's leader to follow through with His commands and directions in the face of doubt, disloyalty and open rebellion. Did Joshua have the mettle to lead by the Book under all circumstances?

Platform of Obedience

Essentially, *be strong and very courageous* was a call for Joshua to make a very firm commitment of unswerving loyalty to God and to all the instructions that He had given to his predecessor. Moses' failure at the borders of Canaan stood as a very clear reminder of how easy it is, at any given moment, for someone to lead from the head and not from the heart. Although the unruly, murmuring multitudes breeched Moses' armor of patience, and provoked the leader to anger, he was still held accountable for not obeying the voice of the Lord.

The repetition of God's command came as a very stern warning to Joshua to make an unalterable commitment to obey God's voice at any cost—be that his reputation or his own life. God's commands have absolutely no room for the "wisdom" of human reason, regardless of how justifiable such reasoning may appear to be. The enemy of God can fill the mind with millions of reasons why anything, other than what God said, could apply or may work. Like the platform of promises, the platform of obedience must be sturdy and very secure.

Joshua was specifically told that he must adhere to everything that Moses had written in the "Book of the Law"—just as Moses commanded Israel to do, shortly before his death (Deuteronomy 4:1, 2). He was not allowed any room to turn to the right or the left. He could not delete or augment one iota of what was written, but had to be very careful *to observe to do according all the law*[1] (Joshua 1:7). What was written was not called suggestions or ideas. They were called laws, indicating that they were expected to be obeyed to the very letter.

Having accepted the position as Israel's new, visible leader, Joshua then had to position himself for success. In this regard, there were no options available to him. The only position opened to him was the one called obedience. He had to make, as it were, a sold-out decision to always stand in a position of obedience to every word of God and his law.

The platform of obedience must be sturdy and very secure.

Israel's success was hinged on Joshua's obedience. *This* people did not know where they were going. They did not have a clue of the art of war, or any working knowledge with regard to the tribes of the land. Without Joshua's confident trust in God's leadership, this great multitude of fickle-minded people would be a source of terror and destruction unto themselves. His unflinching obedience to God was their only hope to find and acquire their place of final settlement and safety. This was the key to their future prosperity and ultimate success in the land of promise.

Position Yourself

Be assured, dear reader, crossing your Jordan can be the most defining moment in your life. What you do on this side of the experience determines what will happen in your life once you make it over to the other side—and you will, just as you have in the past. The reason why you keep coming back to similar frustrating chapters in your life is that you have failed to learn the lessons the Almighty has been trying to teach you. It is my hope that as you thumb through the pages of this book, you will discover the keys that will help to bring you to settlement and success in the future that God holds out to you. One thing is very certain—that is, victory or success does not just happen. It is the consequence of diligent, sustained action on the part of those who attain it

You must position yourself for success, and prayerfully hold that position until success finally comes. However, the quality and soundness of your position is just as important as your diligence in holding on to it. Israel's success came only because Joshua positioned himself in the God who cannot fail; and their prosperity was sustained because it was positioned in the promises made by the God who cannot lie. These are two very important lessons or keys for you to remember.

> **Success is the consequence of diligent, sustained action.**

Positioning strategy is one of the iconic jargons of the business community. It is characterized by two very important marketing qualities—namely, image and impact. A company's image in the marketplace is what defines it from its competitors in the same industry and from all other business entities. Further, it is the impact that that image has in the marketplace that will attract potential consumers to that particular company instead of running to other competitors.

Positioning, therefore, is the ability of a person or business to design and display its image strategically in such a unique, captivating way, that some salient point of the company would occupy an outstanding position (hence the use of the word *positioning*) in the minds of consumers. Most positioning strategies have a tagline aimed at riveting the sticking point of the particular company in the consumers' memory banks. For example, FedEx says, *"the world on time;"* Avis Car Rental says, *"we try harder;"* Kentucky Fried Chicken says, *"finger-lickin' good"* and so on.

Have you ever wondered why it is so easy for even the little youngsters to get their parents to take them to McDonald's once the family car is on the road? The answer is very simple. The sight of McDonald's towering arches has riveted joy and happiness in the minds of children, even before they could even read or pronounce their own names.

On a more personal note, most people make use of a positioning strategy when they want to project a very positive image of themselves in order to obtain something they need, or to impress someone they are trying to influence in some way—for example, the teenager in the quest of a sweetheart; a person going for a job interview; or an athlete trying out for a sports-team, to name a few.

Even God positioned Himself in His Son, Jesus Christ, in order to draw the world to Himself (2 Corinthians 5:19). John 3:16 is God's tagline for a world of sinners who have strayed away from Him to worship at the shrine of the gods of this present world (Romans 1:18-32). In Joshua's case, he did not have to position himself for the job. God called him to be the leader of His people, to take them over the Jordan into the land of promise. Moreover, God gave Joshua the positioning strategy to succeed with the job. He told him to position himself to *observe to do according to all the law.* In other words, *stick to the Book; obey my instruction.* The Almighty also armed Joshua with a captivating tagline that said, *be strong and of a good courage.*

If you are a firm believer in Joshua's God, then your positioning strategy and tagline have already been set for you. It is now up to you to decide whether you are going to follow Joshua's success strategy by positioning yourself in his God, or turn to your own devices. Even a cursive look at your life history will reveal the track record produced by your own ideas and inventions—confusion, disaster, disappointment, headache, heartache and pain.

> **God positioned Himself in Christ to win the world.**
> **We must position ourselves in God win success.**

The Word of God is certainly right when it declares that *there is a way which seems right to a man but its end is the way of death* (Proverbs 16:25). Sometimes the school of hard knocks can be a good teacher, but it holds absolutely no guarantees for those who choose to enroll in it. The God of true wisdom offers you a much better way, even with a life-time assurance policy.

⁵Trust in the LORD with all thine heart; and lean not unto thine own understanding. ⁶In all thy ways acknowledge him, and he shall direct thy paths.

Proverbs 3:5, 6

The Holy Bible has proven, time and again, to be the best counselor and guide for all humankind. This Word of God is just as powerful now as when the Almighty spoke it to bring from nothing our pristine creation and every form of life in it. God and His Word can be trusted more than anyone or anything in this perishing world. For countless centuries they have rebuffed the repeat blows of the critics' hammers, and stood together as a faithful lighthouse in the churning seas of human fears and doubts.

You can trust in the Lord and His Word with all your heart and soul amidst all the chaos of your life and the insecurities of this world. God promises to direct your path if you position yourself to live in obedience to His Word. This calls for inner strength and courage, but these He will supply if you position yourself to lean on Him instead of depending solely upon your own wisdom. Success will certainly come to you when you resist the temptation to do what you feel like doing and surrender to what the revealed will of God—through the spoken or written Word—requires you to do.

Beware of Distractions

. . . do not turn from it to the right or to the left . . .

Everyday life, as it is, is already filled with all types of distractions to pull you away from what you should be doing, consuming your time and energy in following a path that leads to nowhere. When you combine this with what the enemy of your soul casts in your path to get you off track and off message, you have a little glimpse of what you are up against in your pursuit of a blessed life. As you position yourself in God, do not allow the facts about your situation to push you to the right or left in search of solutions when God already has all the answers. Above all, do not make important decisions about your life based on fear that has its source in your human assessment of the factors surrounding that situation.

> **The word of faith is the most invincible weapon against the devil's arsenal of fear and doubt.**

As was stated earlier, fear is a most overwhelming motivator, but it does not originate from God. Rather, it is the most powerful weapon in the devil's arsenal to turn the believer away from God to human reason and short-lived solutions. Remember that facts may only represent human

RUTHVEN J. ROY

perception of your situation and not the real truth, as far as God and His Word are concerned. *Be strong and of a good courage!* Make up your mind to *observe to do all* that is written in the entire Word of God. While fear represents the most powerful tool of the enemy, the Word of faith is the invincible weapon of the Lord of hosts. Paul says that

> *the word of God is <u>quick</u>, and <u>powerful</u>, and <u>sharper than any twoedged sword</u>, piercing even to the dividing asunder of soul and spirit, and of the joints and marrow, and is a discerner of the thoughts and intents of the heart.*

Hebrews 4:12

The apostle also declares that the Word of faith is the believer's impregnable shield of defense against ALL the fiery attacks of the devil (Ephesians 6:16). As a matter of truth, Paul calls it the "above-all-else" piece of armor the believer needs for spiritual warfare. John says it all when he wrote that faith in God and His Word is the ultimate victory over the world and all its situations.

> *[4]For whatever is born of God overcomes the world; and <u>this is the victory that has overcome the world— our faith</u>. [5]Who is the one who overcomes the world,*

but he who believes that Jesus is the Son of God?

1 John 5:4, 5

Therefore, stand firm in your faith in God and His Word. Do not turn to the right or the left, regardless of what you perceive in your environment, and God will come through for you, giving you victory over your world.

Prosperity Regardless

Positioning yourself to walk in obedience to the Lord opens up a whole range of possibilities to you. God told Joshua that no one would be able to stand before him wherever he went—that is, only because He (God) was always in front, and around him. The same will be true for you, because you have positioned yourself in Him. The Bible says that when a man's ways please the Lord, He even makes his enemies show him favor (Proverbs 16:7). "Cash" in on this promise today, for the God of heaven has the ability and resources, unknown to you, to prosper you wherever you go. This prosperity does not only speak of material wealth. It also includes fullness of the blessings of heaven that contribute to abundant life, peace and joy in the Holy Spirit.

Remember, it is the blessings of the Lord that make one rich (Proverbs 10:22), and His prosperity is not subject to any adverse condition on this planet. God has already agreed, and has already made adequate provision to prosper you wherever you go, and under all circumstances. All you have to do is to be steadfast in your position of obedience to Him and His revealed will in His Word. Therefore, be encouraged, beloved reader, with the firm assurance that

whatsoever we ask, we receive of him, because we keep his commandments, and do those things that are pleasing in his sight.

1 John 3:22

Notes:

1. Law here did not only refer to just what was written in the Ten Commandments, but the entire Pentateuch—that is, Genesis to Deuteronomy, the first five books of Moses. At the time, that was the only portion of the Bible that was available to the people of God. The rest came later. While Joshua and the children of Israel had to be directed by the words of the Pentateuch, we today must be guided by the entire Bible, from Genesis to Revelation.

CHAPTER 5

Watch Your Diet: Keep God's Word In Your Mouth

"This book of the law shall not depart from your mouth . . ."

Joshua 1:8

$\mathscr{I}$t is very interesting that God was quite particular regarding what came out of Joshua's mouth as a leader of His people. The directive given in the scripture above, is very calculating because God is fully aware of the tremendous power of words in the ongoing course of the universe. He is the very One who ordered it to be this way. Our entire creation is the product of words that came forth from the mouth of God. The Bible tells us that

> *[6]By the word of the LORD the heavens were made, and by the breath of His mouth all their host. [7]He gathers the waters of the sea together as a heap; He lays up the deeps in storehouses. [8]Let all the earth fear the LORD; let all the inhabitants of the world stand in awe of Him.*

⁹For <u>He spoke</u>, and it was done; <u>He commanded</u>, and it stood fast.

Psalm 33:6-9

Nine times in the Genesis account of creation the Bible repeats the clause, *and God said*, as He spoke everything into being. If there is one being in the universe who truly understands the power of words, especially His Word, it is God Almighty. No doubt, the enemy of our salvation also knows the power of words and he constantly uses that power against us. It is not by chance that he is called *the prince of the power of the air* (Ephesians 2:2). He knows how to take our spoken word, combine them with his demon forces, and use them to spread disaster and destruction in our path. I will deal with this more fully in the latter part of this chapter.

With this brief introduction, we can better appreciate God's very firm command to Joshua to keep the contents of the "Book of the Law" in his mouth; that he should never depart from them. This instruction meant more than just reading the words of the law. God also wanted Joshua to speak the words of the law to himself and to the people continually. Neither Joshua nor the people were to be guided by the words formulated by their own depraved reasoning, for that would only open the door for major human error and deadly satanic influence over the congregation.

> **God gave Joshua a Word-diet to steer him into
> his future destiny.**

It is good to be reminded at this point, that it was flawed human reasoning, and the words such reasoning released from Moses' mouth, that got him into serious trouble on the borders of the Promised Land. Moses failed to follow the words of the Lord and spoke the thoughts of his own mind. His actions were only the result of the combined effect of his thoughts and the words which he spoke. In principle, it was the power of the same combination of the spoken word and human reason that led to the fall of Eve and Adam in the Garden of Eden. The serpent spoke to Eve, and used her to speak to Adam. They both used the power of reason, along with the words spoken to them, to carry out the choices they made.

Therefore, at this major cross-road in Joshua's life, he had to get things right. There was just too much at stake — his future, and that of the entire nation of Israel. Through His commands, God wanted to ensure that Joshua had his tongue under control by giving him a "Word" diet to guide him into his future destiny. Joshua had to order his life by the confession of his mouth. God wanted no less. In other words, God was saying: "Speak My words only and you will have great success. Do otherwise and you will corrupt yourself and all those who follow you" (my paraphrase).

God knows that it is quite easy for our thoughts to be influenced by whatever is happening in our immediate environment, and that our speech is the product of our thoughts. Thus, He wanted to save Joshua that trouble. Don't waste the time thinking about the situation before you, Joshua; just keep the words of the law pouring out of your mouth.

What's in Your Mouth?

Table etiquette informs us that it is not proper to chew food with one's mouth opened, because viewing the contents of a person's mouth when he is eating is surely not a pretty sight. It is very easy for someone to lose his appetite for his favorite dish if another person deliberately, or unknowingly, violates this simple table protocol. Well, the contents of this section do not have anything to do with the everyday food you place in your mouth. It goes much deeper.

The question that forms the sub-heading is intended for your thoughtful reflection upon the words which form the gist of your everyday conversation and that have influenced the course of your life. Yes, you read right. Words spoken can determine the course of your life. The sad truth is that the Jordan situation that may be raging in your life right now may have been started by words you have spoken into your life, or words spoken into you by someone. Let's take a little closer look.

The power of your tongue

When I was a youngster, I was taught to ignore the bruising words of others by repeating the following "band-aid" idioms or proverbs: "Sticks and stones may break my bones, but words will never hurt me;" "words are wind, but blows are unkind." Although my siblings and I rehearsed and repeated these lines countless times with the hope of warding off the verbal attacks of our peers, we would often burst into uncontrollable tears when we related these hurtful incidents to our parents.

Words hurt more than sticks and stones.

As children, we knew that our parents' well-meaning fixes did not work, because we hurt so badly on the inside. Some are still carrying deeply inflicted wounds from their childhood and require professional help to relieve the pressure of the pain they feel on the inside. Indeed "sticks and stones may break my bones, but their pain will go away; hurtful words no bones will break, but their scars prolong their stay."[1]

Today, we know so much more about the power of our words—spoken or written—that those childhood idioms are no longer tenable or repeated in our modern societies. In fact we have developed alternative proverbs to counteract the effect of those misguided idioms of the past. For example, "words cut more than swords;" "the pen is mightier than the sword;" and "words have no wings but they can fly a thousand miles."

Postmodern civilizations have also put in place laws to protect their citizens from the inappropriate use of words—those designed to hurt, malign, degrade, or destroy one's character or reputation. Many lawsuits charge the perpetrators of these laws with libel. Verbal abuse is given just as much (and in some cases even more) weight as physical abuse in the average court of law, for we know today that words are more than wind and are capable of doing much more harm than blows.

The Bible says that the human tongue has the power to speak life or death in a person, situation or thing (Proverbs 18:21). James' description of this power is even more frightening and needs to be studied very carefully.

⁵So also the tongue is a small part of the body, and yet it boasts of great things. See how great a forest is set aflame by such a small fire! ⁶And the tongue is a fire, the very world of iniquity; the tongue is set among our members as that which defiles the entire body, and sets on fire the course of our life, and is set on fire by hell. ⁷For every species of beasts and birds, of reptiles and creatures of the sea, is tamed and has

been tamed by the human race. <u>⁸But no one can tame</u>
<u>the tongue; it is a restless evil and full of deadly</u>
<u>poison</u>. ⁹With it we bless our Lord and Father, and
with it we curse men, who have been made in the
likeness of God; ¹⁰from the same mouth come both
blessing and cursing.

James 3:5-10

> **Our tongue has the capacity to shape the course of**
> **our entire life**

The Bible compares the human tongue to an uncontrollable fire; a world full of iniquity, possessing the capacity to defile the whole body and set a person's entire life ablaze. What is even most disconcerting is the truth that the powerful fire of the tongue is kindled directly from the pit of hell (v. 6). The scariest thing about kindling is that once the fire begins to rage, the kindling itself is consumed and can no longer be found. How true this is also of the deadly words released by an iniquitous tongue. Quite often, of course, the evil words spoken may have long been forgotten, while the afflicted individual searches in vain to find the kindling that ignited the painful, disastrous situation that is raging in his life.

How many children's lives are in chaos because of

the unbridled tongue of their frustrated, angry and unsuspecting parents. The same holds true for parents, spouses, friends, neighbors, relatives and others in every walk of life. The Bible says that we are snared by the words of our mouth (Proverbs 6:2); and that *a fool's mouth is his destruction, and his lips are the snare of his soul* (Proverbs 18:7). This restless evil, called the tongue, is full of deadly poison (James 3:8) and has the power, through its lethal venom, to infect and destroy our lives and the lives of those we love. The poison released by the tongue has the power to produce fear, anger, envy, distrust, malice, sickness, disease and death; and whosoever loves it will eat its fruits (Proverbs 18:21).

The Word of God makes it clear that our tongue has the capacity to shape the course of our entire life (James 3:6); but the tongue is only the servant of another corrupt master—that is, our deceitful heart. Let's take a closer look at this. Jesus once told the wicked, self-righteous religious leaders of His day:

[33]Either make the tree good, and his fruit good; or else make the tree corrupt, and his fruit corrupt: for the tree is known by his fruit. [34]O generation of vipers, how can ye, being evil, speak good things? <u>for out of the abundance of the heart the mouth speaketh</u>. [35]A good man out of the good treasure of the heart bringeth forth good things: and an evil man out of the

evil treasure bringeth forth evil things.

Matthew 12:33-35, KJV

**The only way to control the power of the tongue
is through a converted, consecrated heart.**

The point Christ makes is very simple and straightforward. The tongue can only speak of that which fills the heart or spiritual core of person. He compares this moral center of the individual to a tree or a treasure house that is capable of producing good or evil fruits, or good or evil things. The Bible also says that the heart of the un-regenerated man is the most deceitful thing in the entire world. *The heart is deceitful above all things, and desperately wicked: who can know it?* (Jeremiah 17:9, KJV). The implied answer to the rhetorical question at the end of the verse is, of course, *no one.* This pernicious quality of the unconverted heart is what makes the human tongue such a deadly instrument.

The only way to control the power of a fiery tongue is through the avenue of a converted and consecrated heart. We are able to direct our tongue by diligently training our heart and mind to obey the infallible Word of God. Our minds must be renewed constantly by the life-giving Word of truth. This is what keeps the heart from deceitfulness and corruption. We are counseled in the book of Proverbs: *"Keep thy heart with all diligence; for out of it are the issues of life"* (Proverbs 4:23). So what's in your mouth, dear reader? That depends on what you have deposited in your heart and mind. King David rightly confessed: *Your word I have treasured in my heart, that I may not sin against You* (Psalm 119:11). Therefore, you must keep the Word of God in your heart, so that your mind will always be controlled by the thoughts of God and not your own. Then, out of the abundance of your heart, your mouth will be filled with the Word of God.

Stop Helping the Devil!

[11]Put on the full armor of God, so that you will be able to stand firm against the schemes of the devil. [12]For our struggle is not against flesh and blood, but against the rulers, against the powers, against the world forces of this darkness, against the spiritual forces of wickedness in the heavenly places.

Ephesians 6:11, 12

The Word of God contains many aliases for the devil—Lucifer, Satan, evil one, prince of this world, serpent, and dragon, to name a few—and each one of them points to a different mode of operation by the wily foe. However, the alias that is of particular interest in this section is the one dubbed "prince of the power of the air" (Ephesians 2:2). This devious, hateful enemy marshals all his demon forces of the underworld and unleashes them to wreak havoc in earthly and heavenly atmospheres.

These catastrophic activities are not limited to phenomena as storms, hurricanes, tornadoes, typhoons and such like, but also to the words released by the human tongue. Yes, the devil has the ability to use our words against us by magnifying their capacity through the operations of his atmospheric demonic forces.

Words are not simply the product of air pushed out from our lungs and formed by the use of our tongue and teeth. They are also filled with energy and power to create and destroy things in this world and our lives. History reveals that words have demonstrated their power to defeat armies and to inspire nations; to win an election or to lose a candidacy; to engender war or to bring about peace; to arouse hope or to create despair; to administer comfort or to cause severe pain; to hasten the call of death or to breathe new life.[2]

The enemy of your soul is quite aware of the power of your words, even though spoken in jest. He does not care whether your words were meant to be a prank, funny, or anything else. He is out for destruction and certainly will not spare you the pain because you were only making a joke. He will take the advantage to use anything you say against you.

How many times does one have to turn around and eat the very words one has spoken, whether in jest or deliberately? The Bible warns: *Do not let any unwholesome talk come out of your mouths, but only what is helpful for building others up according to their needs, that it may benefit those who listen* (Ephesians 4:29, NRSV).

We cannot afford to help the enemy, or render him the slightest advantage. Paul said that we should not give the devil any opportunity (Ephesians 4:27), and certainly not by the words we speak. In order to do this, we must educate our hearts daily with the Word of God, and discipline ourselves to get rid of our negative list of name-calling, curses, bad wishes and more, which we speak on ourselves, spouses, children and others. Here are a few examples:

1. Instead of saying, "*my feet or head is killing me*," simply say, "*my feet are tired,*" or "*my head hurts.*"
2. Instead of saying, "*I am sick and tired . . . ,*" why not simply say, "*I am frustrated?*" "*I am angry or upset?*" "*I am disappointed?*"
3. Instead of saying, "*It blew my mind,*" you can say something like, "*it was astounding,*" "*incredible,*" or simply "*almost impossible to believe.*"
4. Instead of saying, "*I am dying to see you,*"

simply say, "*I long to see you.*"

5. Instead of speaking something negative on your child, spouse or anyone else in order to elicit some positive conduct, speak your positive expectation of the behavior you would like to see in the person and keep right on reinforcing it.

Now, here is a true story to illustrate the point I am making. This very unfortunate incident occurred while I was visiting my home country of Trinidad and Tobago, nestled among the beautiful islands of the Caribbean Sea. A Christian mother and her son, from the sister island of Tobago, were involved in a money partnership called a *su-su*³ (also called a box or partner-hand, in some of the other islands). When the time came for the son to draw his *hand*, his mother gave him a sum of $9,700.00.

Unknowing to her, the young man took the money and "invested" almost the total amount (I believe it was about $9,500) in a very large gold chain—the *bling-bling* kind that hangs very low. Needless to say, the mother was very upset by her son's poor judgment and consistently chided him about his chain. In her efforts to have him get rid of the gold chain, she repeatedly warned her son, who was planning a trip to Trinidad: "If you go to Trinidad with that chain on your neck they will kill you." "You'd better leave that chain home."

Of course, the disobedient son did not spend $9,500 on his *bling-bling* to leave it at home. When the time finally arrived for him to travel to the sister island, he apparently pretended to leave home without the chain, but by the time he was out of the door it was around his neck. The ferry took about two and a half hours to get to Trinidad, and when he got there he was expecting to meet with his brother at a place called Curepe.

However, that very night, about one hour after he disembarked from the ferry, some young men, under the influence of satanic forces, accosted him and demanded his chain. He tried to fight them off and began to run away; but one of them whipped out a gun and shot him. The report said that he died while still clinging to the chain about his neck.

When I read this story in the newspaper the following day, I was heart-broken. This young man could have died in Tobago, his home country, and by any other means than by being murdered for a chain. Instead he died exactly like his mother said—murdered at the hands of robbers in Trinidad. Many may think this was co-incidental, but I believe differently, because I stand by the Word which says that death and life are in the power of the tongue (Proverbs 18:21).

In Christ, every promise of God is already fulfilled.

Who is to say that if this unsuspecting mother had spoken God's promise of protection over her son instead of the death-dealing words of the enemy, that the outcome would not have been very different? You cannot give place to the devil in any situation, for he will not forgive your innocence or ignorance. Had it not been for the prevailing mercy of God, we would have been all dead a very long time ago. Yet, we dare not presume on God's mercy by being very careless with the words which come out of our mouths.

Position yourself to fill your mouth and life with the precious promises of the Word of God instead of the negative words associated with your upbringing. Then watch the miracles unfold as God opens a way in the midst of your Jordan for you to walk right through to your appointed destiny. In Christ, every promise of God is already fulfilled; so speak them over your life and all your situations.

For all the promises of God in him are yea, and in him Amen, unto the glory of God by us.

2 Corinthians 1:20

Please notice that the Bible says "ALL" God's promises already have "YES" and "AMEN" attached to them because they are already underwritten in the blood of Jesus, our Savior. Therefore, search for them in the Word of God and feast (meditate) on them till they become a part of your daily vocabulary. Then replace your words of fear, doubt and negativity with faith-filled promises and watch the living words of God work for you.

The prophet Jeremiah confessed: *"Thy words were found, and I did eat them; and thy word was unto me the joy and rejoicing of mine heart: for I am called by thy name, O LORD God of hosts"* (Jeremiah 15:16). David said, *"how sweet are thy words unto my taste! yea, sweeter than honey to my mouth!"* (Psalm 119:103).

Don't you think it is time for you to change the contents of your mouth? David invites you to do so right now. He says, *"O taste and see that the LORD is good: blessed is the man that trusteth in him* (Psalm 34:8). Try it. Open your mouth and taste the incomparable sweetness that flows from the fountain of God's good promises in His Word. I guarantee that you will certainly love it; for there is absolutely nothing in this world that can match the satisfaction and joy which this experience brings.

Notes:

1. Ruthven J. Roy, Adaptation of "sticks and stones" idiom.
2. Ruthven J. Roy, *Imitating God: The Amazing Secret of Living His Life.*

3. A simple *su-su* consists of a group of people who come together in a monetary partnership over a specific period of time in order to achieve some financial leverage. Each person is required to contribute to the money pot a stated sum of cash—called a *hand*—on a weekly, bi-weekly or monthly basis, depending on what the group agreed upon when the *su-su* began. An individual is able to draw in advance from the pot, depending on when he requires his *hand*, the sum total of all his contributions over the term life of the *su-su*. *Hands* are paid out weekly, bi-weekly or monthly to an assigned person, according to the terms of the verbal or written *su-su* contract, until the last hand is distributed. *Su-su* may vary in complexity depending on the number of people, term life, and the types of hands— half-hand, hand and a half, double-hand, etc.

4. *Hand* refers to both the periodic amount of cash each person places into the *su-su* pot, and also to the sum total of those contributions which he receives at the time of his drawing from the pot.

CHAPTER 6

Change Your Thinking: Program Your Soul For Success

". . . you shall <u>meditate on it day and night</u>, so that you may be careful to do according to all that is written in it . . ."

Joshua 1:8

From all accounts, God was not depending on man's wisdom to provide reliable and responsible leadership for His people. He intended to bring them safely through the Jordan into the land that He had promised to their forefathers. Leading Israel His way was the only guarantee for their success. Therefore, it was worth God's time and effort to give Joshua detailed instructions with regard to this mission.

To facilitate this purpose, God required this newly appointed leader to have a complete working knowledge of all that was written in the Book of the Law. This Book, which contained the expressed will of Jehovah, was given not only to shape the contents of Joshua's mouth, but also to train His mind to think God's thoughts. Joshua's speech had to be controlled by his sense of being and also his thinking.

The power of human reason does not determine the outcome of everything, because not everything we think is right or fruitful. As a matter of fact, it was the devil's breeching of human reason that plunged the race into the horrific nightmare of sin. Ever since the "Fall," mankind has depended on human intellect more than on the Word of the Living God. Thus, human reason has become the greatest snare of every living soul. The Bible confirms that *there is a way which seems right to a man, but its end is the way of death* (Proverbs 16:25). Intellectual reasoning is neither failsafe nor reliable, but short-sighted and blind. Therefore, it cannot stand on its own as the moral compass of humankind.

The power of human reason does not determine everything.

Consequently, Joshua's sense of being, not just his thinking, had to be shifted away from himself to the Almighty. In other words, the spirit of the man must be in control of the thinking of the man. Scripture says that *the spirit of man is the lamp of the Lord, which searches [searching] all the innermost parts of his being* (Proverb 20:27). God had to capture Joshua's spirit and mind to equip him fully for his life assignment. Nothing else would suffice.

There are so many Christian leaders whose minds are not filled with the Word of God, but the wisdom of men.

Even though the Word is in their mouths, their spirits are far away from the God who gave it. They are so puffed up with pride, and wrapped up in their knowledge that God cannot use them to take his people over their Jordans, to the place of rest He ordained for them. The Word of God correctly states that *as a man [he] thinketh in his heart, so is he: Eat and drink, saith he to thee; but his heart is not with thee* (Proverbs 23:7).

A person is quite capable of thinking and expressing one thing from his head, while his heart or spirit is far from whatever that thought is. The word "heart" here refers to more than just the brain. Its deeper reference is to a person's moral center or spirit core. If a person's spirit is not right, then his thinking and speaking will follow in its trail.

God's Objective

While the mistake and death of his predecessor, Moses, lay fresh on Joshua's mind, God capitalized upon the moment to make the indelible impression upon him about the gravity of his role as Israel's new leader. He told Joshua to meditate day and night upon all that Moses had written in the Book of the Law. It is quite easy to miss the full force of this simple statement, so we must take a little time to consider it very carefully. Meditation carries the idea not only of deep contemplation, but also of life application.

In meditation, we ponder upon an idea, a truth, a supposition, a being or any other thing of personal interest, while at the same time correlating the object of our meditation to our own life. In Joshua's case, the focus of his meditation was God and all that He commanded in the Book of the Law. He was instructed to pursue this spiritual discipline day and night. Put another way, he was to do this all the time.

What was God's objective for this carefully-worded directive? The Almighty was seeking to condition Joshua's spirit and mind with His words and His thoughts so that they would become his first (not second) natural response in executing his leadership function over the children of Israel. God wanted Joshua to be so filled with His Spirit and His words so that when he spoke or acted, it would be as though the Almighty Himself was speaking or acting on behalf of His people.

A person's spirit and mind must be programmed for success.

In so doing, Joshua was going to be the unstoppable force God had commissioned him to be in the earth. No one was going to be able to stand before him all the days of his life (Joshua 1:5). The annals of Israel's successful crossing over the Jordan, and of their settlement in the Promise Land, testify to the outcome of God's leadership in the life of Joshua.

Getting Profitable Results

Someone wisely described insanity as the syndrome of people doing the same thing over and over, and over again and expecting different results. There are also those people who go down the maze of life "hemming" and "hawing" about everything or everyone they think is responsible for moving their proverbial "cheese," instead of "sniffing" and "scurrying" around to find a new block.[1] Many people do not adapt well to change, but life is inundated with it. The preceding chapter already shows how the words of your lips have the power to influence the course of your life. The raging Jordan you are facing right now may have been initiated by some negative word released by your untamed tongue.

You now have the opportunity to change the direction of your life. Since your tongue has the power to set on fire the course of your life (James 3:6), it also possesses the ability to put the fire out if you learn how to harness the power of that little member of your body. Adopting God's preparation strategy for Joshua is a very good place to start if you want to bring profitable results to your life. However, changing the course of your life is not achieved by solely focusing on what is coming out of your mouth. You must add the indispensable component of meditating on what is written in the Book of the Law—the Bible.

Soul-Food Diet

Whenever we hear the word "diet" we instinctively begin thinking about weight management, exercise routine or some prevailing medical condition. This time, however, it is not so. In the context of our present discourse, I do not want to focus your attention on the types of food with which you feed your body—important as these are. I want to center your interest on the diet of your soul. It is your spiritual diet that stores the precious treasures of God's Word in your spirit, and which influences what type of words will escape through your lips. Jesus once had this to say to the Jewish leaders:

> [34]*O generation of vipers, how can ye, being evil, speak good things? for out of the abundance of the heart the mouth speaketh.* [35]*A good man out of the good treasure of the heart bringeth forth good things: and an evil man out of the evil treasure bringeth forth evil things.*

Matthew 12:34, 35

Essentially, what Jesus is saying is that if person's spiritual core or moral center (heart) is evil, it would be reflected in the things which he says; for the mouth speaks forth from the abundance of that which fills the heart. He also hints that whatever an individual feeds his soul is stored in the treasure-house of his heart. It is from that moral center that every thought, word or action, good or evil, emerges.

Hence, God did not tell Joshua to focus only on keeping what was written in the Book of the Law in his mouth. He went a step further by insisting that Joshua meditate day and night upon the contents of the Book as well. This approach was to ensure that Joshua would be able to do all that God required of him. The purpose of meditation is not just about being in a contemplative mode, but about probing the inner life of the seeker to bring it into alignment with the focus of the meditation.

Ultimately, mediation is about bringing about change in one's thinking and lifestyle. Joshua had to program his spirit and mind with the Book of the Law so that he would be able to live by every word of God, and diligently teach the same to the people under his care.

Are you eating the right stuff?

In the context of the ongoing deliberation, your speech is a reflection of your diet. What have you been feeding to your soul over the years of your life—junk food, or wholesome provisions from the Living Word of God? What is your feeding source? That is quite easy to tell. Just examine the contents of your mouth and you will see that they correlate with the place you go shopping to feed your hungry soul on a daily basis. The children of Israel often ran into very difficult times with God and themselves because of their feeding patterns. See how God explained the depth of their folly. He said:

> *"For My people have committed two evils: They have forsaken Me, The fountain of living waters, to hew for themselves cisterns, broken cisterns that can hold no water."*

Jeremiah 2:13

Have you run into hard times because you have committed the same two evils described above? Are you among the numberless throng who tries to operate life without God, or who has placed God and His Word as footnote items on their shopping list? If you are in a current Jordan situation, it may be because the cistern from which you have been drinking is broken. Moreover, if the contents of your mouth are getting in the way of your progress, it is time to change your diet. You need to begin shopping somewhere else. Why not try the Fountain of Living Waters? By the way, how much do you spend for your food? Is it costing you too much and taking you nowhere? Well, I have very exciting and comforting news for you. God has a very special program that would certainly benefit you. Read what He says:

> *[1]"Ho! Everyone who thirsts, come to the waters; And you who have no money come, buy and eat. Come, buy wine and milk Without money and without cost. [2]Why do you spend money for what is not bread, And your wages for what does not satisfy? Listen carefully to Me, and eat what is good, And delight yourself in abundance. [3]Incline your ear and come to Me. Listen, that you may live; And I will make an everlasting covenant with you."*

Isaiah 55:1-3

First of all, God is trying to get your attention. He says, "Ho!" In modern-day terms, God is touting: "Hey, look over here!" "Come!" He is calling for everyone, and that includes you—that is, if you are thirsty and longing for something better. The good thing about turning to God's shopping outlet is that He offers to everyone His "all-you-can-eat" buffet for free. No one in his right mind would pass up on a deal like

RUTHVEN J. ROY

this. I love shopping for free, especially in the middle of this Jordan-type economy. I don't know about you.

Secondly, God even pleads with you, as He does with everyone else, "Why waste your money on things that do not really bring any lasting satisfaction to your life?" He invites you to eat what is good and available to you in abundance so that you may enjoy a truly happy and fruitful life. Finally, God ends His sales pitch with the promise to make an everlasting covenant with you and everyone who chooses Him as their one-stop shopping Source. He guarantees your complete satisfaction by placing His name and character on the line.

Center Your Soul

⁵Trust in the LORD with all thine heart; and lean not unto thine own understanding. ⁶In all thy ways acknowledge him, and he shall direct thy paths. ⁷Be not wise in thine own eyes: fear the LORD, and depart from evil. ⁸It shall be health to thy navel, and marrow to thy bones

Proverbs 3:5-8

If God is going to be your Source, you must learn how to center your soul on Him right now. You must feed your spirit with His Word so that the Spirit of truth can re-wire your logic box (mind) and the circuit of your soul to make God the auto-Pilot of your life. Self has to be dethroned in this process. Additionally, your mind must be renewed in its condition, receptivity and function through consistent, contemplative study of what is written in the Book (Romans 12:2).

The Bible is a living life-book, not a textbook.

No longer must self and human wisdom be in the driver's seat in your life, for that will only perpetuate chaos and disaster. Now is the time for your day-and-night meditation on the Word, so that you will be able to know what God will have you do when you confront your Jordan. Let God do all the driving in your life and He will not only direct your path, but also eliminate your stress and restore your health.

The Word of God has perfect directions and promises for every imaginable situation in your life, but you must discipline yourself to meditate upon its enduring, life-changing precepts in order to reap its rich benefits. The Bible is a living life-book. Stop relating to it like a textbook. It is not a book that you just pick up when you are going to church, or when you are in a dire strait and need the help of Jehovah.

These words of the Almighty are living and very

powerful, and must be the order of the day for every day of
your life. You live by every word that proceeds from the
mouth of God—the One who created all life. This Word of
God is guaranteed to change your life if you take the time to
eat and meditate upon it day and night. Pay very close
attention to what God is saying to you in the scripture below:

> My son, _give attention to my words;_ Incline your ear
> to my sayings. _²¹Do not let them depart from your_
> _sight; Keep them in the midst of your heart._ ²²For they
> are life to those who find them and health to all their
> body. ²³Watch over your heart with all diligence, for
> from it flow the springs of life.

Proverbs 4:20-23

Pay attention!

The very first thing God says is "Pay attention." In
other words, "Turn off and turn away from all other
distractions, and look to Me." "Where is the Book of the
Law?" "Are you able to locate it?" Once you've found it, it
must become the front and center of your daily focus. The
Word of God must move from being non-existent, or a side-
bar in your life, and become the mainstay of your earthly
existence. It must become the abiding point of reference for

your every decision.

I know that there may be many things going on in the world and in your head that are crying out for your attention and attracting your interest, but God says to you right now: "Pay attention, because I can and will take care of you and all that's going on in your life with one word from My lips." "Do not permit yourself to be distracted from Me; pay attention to My words and live!"

Who's got your ears?

During the last presidential election in the United States of America, it became quite obvious to the general public that first lady, Michele Obama, had, and still has, the president's ear. Before Barak became the first African-American president of the United States of America, Michele was the confidant not only to Barak's political concerns, but to his personal and social concerns as well. It is very unlikely that that will ever change.

In the general scheme of things, however, everyone has someone whose advice he/she is pretty much always open to listen to—be that a spouse, parent, pastor, guardian, teacher or very close friend, to name a few. Who's got your ears when you are in the thick of your raging Jordan? It is not strange that many people have one person or set of persons who has their ears in the time of pleasure, and a totally different group or individual when they are in the midst of their pain. However, life has taught some of us that the opinions of many of the people who had our ears were not worth a dime. Nevertheless, there are many individuals who have yet to figure that out.

God's good news to you right now is that He wants to be your confidant. He does not only want your attention; He wants you to listen very carefully to what He has to say to you in His Word. Be assured, God does not speak empty words and all His promises are "yea and amen"—they are already signed, sealed and waiting to be delivered, post-paid from Calvary, to you.

Through the prophet Isaiah, He said that not one word uttered by His lips will return to Him without first accomplishing that for which He had assigned it (Isaiah 55:10, 11). He is the God who cannot lie (Titus 1:2), for once He says something, that something becomes whatever He says. You would do well to allow the Almighty to have your ear always, for then you are certain that you can trust Him and never be afraid. He will surely direct all your goings out and coming in, from this time forth and forevermore (Psalm 121:8).

What are you staring at?

How often along the road of life have we encountered

someone who was dressed in a very peculiar way, or was doing something out of the ordinary that really caught our attention, to have them shout back at us: "What are you staring at?" Much to our surprise and embarrassment we musingly turn away without answering, and go on our merry way thinking, "what a weirdo!"

There is just so much to stare at in our crazy, twisted world where nothing seems wrong anymore—the television, movie, computer, and video-game screens; weird body piercings, tattoos and hairdos; fancy neon lights, automobiles, and even the Dow Jones Index—the lists are endless.

Caught in the sea of all this, may I ask you, "What's grabbing your attention?" "What are you staring at right now?" Is it failing finances, failing health, failing job, failing mortgage, failing children, failing marriage? Everything seems to be failing these days. Maybe you are staring in another direction, at something you think holds a bright future for you. "What is it?" "What are you really staring at?"

How many times have you been around the block of life and ended up staring at the same rotten situation? Well, some things won't change because you have been around block, and other things will never change unless you change your direction, or change your block. In this one passage of scripture quoted above (Proverbs 4:20-23), God is seeking to bring your entire life together for you—all through the power of His Holy Word. He said that you ought not to allow His Word to depart from your sight (v. 21).

I cannot emphasize enough the vital importance of keeping God's Word ever before you, especially in this present crisis environment. Everyone is running around looking for answers to their most vexing problems, when the answers are already right at hand in the Word of the living God. If they would only take the time to keep the focus of their eyes in the Book, their vision will get clearer as God's Spirit fills them with wisdom and insight to chart new directions for their lives. It is time to stop staring at the problems or into naked space, while only glancing or wondering about the Word. Get engaged with the Book, and watch God open a dry path through your Jordan for you.

Heart condition

We have come to very depressing times in the history of our world. The fallen economy has filled the minds and hearts of the masses with fear and apprehension over the future. Stress, hypertension, depression and heart-failure have spiked upward, and murder-suicides have become very common occurrences among those who were once labeled as well-to-do. People have suddenly become aware that the things on which they had hung their life's hopes and dreams, and their family's future were false, and they have grown to be so terribly afraid because they have no other form of real security.

The Word of God is very accurate in predicting that in these last days there will be distress among the nations of the world and people's hearts will fail because they are so afraid of what the future holds (Luke 21:25, 26).

Fear, which leads to stress, is the product of a mind that has lost its bearing on the truth about life. The human mind does not respond very well to stress, and the humanistic philosophies do not have the answers to bring abiding peace to the teeming multitudes of troubled souls who now roam our planet. The world's systems have proven inadequate to stem the overwhelming tide of human suffering and woe.

Center yourself in the Word of God, and hold to that position

How are you coping? What's the condition of your mind and heart—both physical organ and moral center? Do the conditions of our world and your present Jordan fill you with despair? Well, God's answer to your aching heart and troubled spirit is His life-giving Word. The scripture we have been reviewing, invites you to keep the Word of God in the core of your heart and it would preserve your life in the time of deep distress. In other words, center yourself in the Word of God, and hold to that position.

Meditating on God's Word will bring a sense of His presence through the ministry of the Holy Spirit, and you will experience His peace. The things the world offers through its various systems cannot bring peace to the human soul. Only God and His Word can. The prophet Isaiah says that God will keep you in perfect peace if you can keep your mind focused on Him (Isaiah 26:3). He will guard your heart and mind against the ravages of this stressful, earthly existence. Read this precious counsel from the Word:

> *⁶Do not be anxious about anything, but in everything, by prayer and petition, with thanksgiving, present your requests to God. ⁷And the peace of God, which transcends all understanding, will guard your hearts and your minds in Christ Jesus.*

> Philippians 4:6, 7, NIV

It is quite obvious that God wants the total person to be fully engaged with the instructions which He has deposited in His precious Word. Such engagement, He says, will add to the length and quality of life, and restore health and wholeness to the entire body. In other words, the Holy Bible is a total life and fitness package that is second to nothing else that this world has to offer.

King David, the psalmist, says that the person who

meditates day and night on the Word of God will be *like a tree planted*—that's stability and security; *by the rivers of water*—that's continuous refreshment; *that bringeth forth his fruits in his season*—that's on-time fruitfulness; *his leaf also shall not wither*—that's ultimate protection; *and whatsoever he doeth shall prosper*—that's unlimited prosperity (Psalm 1:2, 3).

The Bible is God's total life and fitness package

What else can anyone ask for? The everlasting Word of God is the infallible manual for life on this planet. Those who try to operate without it will eventually become human wreckage, if God does not extend His mercy to save them from complete destruction. Why take the risk, when the Word offers a whole range of possibilities for your life? Embrace God's free offer and live a quality, fruitful life. Remember, you live by every word which proceeds from the mouth of Jehovah. Therefore, hold to the Word and never let it go.

Like VISA, MasterCard, or your cellular phone, you must never leave home without the Word in your soul. Always power-up and program your soul every day before you get on the road, or become busily engaged with all that this earthly life throws at you. If you meditate faithfully upon the precepts and promises of this Book of Life, it will change the way you think, speak and live; and will make you an unstoppable success story in this world, while preparing you for the world to come.

Notes:

1. Thoughts from Spencer Johnson's *Who Moved My Cheese?* (New York: Putnam, 1998).

CHAPTER 7

Apply God's Wisdom: Design Your Success

. . . for then <u>thou shalt make</u> thy way prosperous, and then thou shalt have <u>good success</u>.

Joshua 1:8, KJV

*O*ne cannot help but notice that God places the outcome of Joshua's success in life squarely upon the shoulders of the newly-appointed leader. As far as God was concerned, Joshua's success was already a completed item on His calendar of events, because He had already commanded it. The rest was totally up to Joshua. Consequently, God reminded His appointee, "*<u>Have I not commanded you</u>? Be strong and courageous! Do not tremble or be dismayed, for <u>the Lord your God is with you wherever you go</u>*" (Joshua 1:9).

Whenever God commands a thing, it is already a done deal. A very short time prior to his appointment, while the children of Israel camped in the plains of Moab just before the Jordan crossing, Balak, king of the Moabites, hired the prophet Balaam to curse the blessed people of God. After mercifully getting by his speaking donkey and the angel of the Lord with the flaming sword, Balaam tried to curse Israel on three separate occasions, from three different angles (really places). However, try as he did, he could not turn back the word of blessing that the Lord had placed in his mouth. As a matter of fact, the second time that Balaam opened his mouth to curse Israel, the very first utterance to meet the King Balak's ears was:

> *"God is not a man, that He should lie, nor a son of man, that He should repent; Has He said, and will He not do it? Or has He spoken, and will He not make it good?"*

Numbers 23:19

Whenever God commands a thing, it is already a done deal.

God does not have to tell a lie (or "suck up," in modern phraseology) for fear of not pleasing someone; nor does He have to say He is sorry for not doing something that He had promised. He is God Almighty, and who can fault Him on anything that He has promised or spoken? In the very next verse, Balaam went on to tell the king; *"Behold, I have received a command to bless; when He has blessed, then I cannot revoke it"* (verse 20). Moreover, the third time King

Balak took Balaam to curse God's children; the prophet did not even waste the time to seek another sign from God. The Bible says that when he lifted up his eyes and saw the orderly formation of Israel camping tribe by tribe in the plains below, the Spirit of God came upon him and he took up another round of blessing upon them (Numbers 24:1-3). He even ended his discourse with the follow blessing: *"Blessed is everyone who blesses you, and cursed is everyone who curses you"* (verse 9).

Be assured, whoever God blesses, no one can curse! And the words of Jehovah are more certain to come to pass than the sun is expected to rise in the east and set in the west. It is easier for the heavens and the earth, as we know them, to pass away than for one word of God to fail (Mark 13:31).

Joshua's Success

The Almighty had established all the necessary conditions for Joshua to succeed in his appointed task of taking the children of Israel over the Jordan, to possess the inheritance which He had promised their forefathers. Now, it was up to Joshua to follow through on God's prescription for his success, or ignore them altogether by pursuing the dictates of his own mind. Since the writing of this volume is in retrospect of Joshua's unequaled accomplishments, it is very safe to say that this successor of Moses accepted God's instructions and took responsibility for the outcome of his appointed destiny.

Whoever God blesses, no one can curse.

Looking back, it can be said that Joshua was strong and very courageous because he leaned on God's power and ability as the source of his confidence and victory. Joshua also spent considerable time reading, meditating upon, and speaking all that was written by his predecessor in the Book of the Law. The Word of the Almighty was in his spirit, in his mouth and in his life and practice. God had promised Joshua that should he pursue diligently and unreservedly all that was delivered to him through Moses, *he (Joshua) would make his way prosperous* and shall have *good success.* Joshua's life of progressive victory and unequaled success showed that he was careful to do all that was written in the Word of God.

Meditation influences attitude; attitude influences lifestyle and performance; and performance determines one's success or failure. Because Joshua programmed his spirit and mind with the Word of the living God, the process shaped his thought-life and influenced every decision he made. Meditating on the Word connected this man of God to the thoughts of the Almighty, and placed him in a position to apply heaven-born wisdom on his way to uninterrupted success. Certainly, whatsoever God thinks and speaks MUST come to pass. It's that simple. The Bible says that whatsoever is born of God—person, thought, word or act—overcomes the world and all its contrary forces; and this is the victory that overcomes the world, even our faith (1 John 5:4).

Joshua's faith connected him intrinsically to the Source of good success—the God of his forefathers. As a result, the course and end result of his life testify of his remarkable and unparalleled achievements through the grace and blessings of the Almighty. Chapters 23 and 24 of the book written by this inspired servant of God give a good review of the glowing results. Permit me to draw your attention once again to Joshua's parting words. It is my hope and prayer that you may be inspired by them.

"Now behold, today I am going the way of all the earth, and you know in all your hearts and in all your souls that not one word of all the good words which the LORD your God spoke concerning you has failed; all have been fulfilled for you, not one of them has failed."

Joshua 23:14

> **Meditation influences attitude; attitude influences lifestyle; and lifestyle determines one's success or failure.**

God Has Spoken

Believe it or not, God has already spoken many things pertaining to your success in life, and every principle regarding those things are carefully chronicled in the Book of the Law—the Holy Bible. Moreover, whatsoever God has spoken or written is already completed as far as He is concerned. All that is left for you to do is to seek and follow diligently His wise counsel in His Word so that you can achieve *good* success.

Remember that *good* success does not depend on your station in life, or on the nature of your past or present circumstances, but on your yielding to the prevailing presence and influence of the Almighty who is with you. He has written your future destiny, and holds it securely in the palm of His omnipotent hand. Trust Him to guide you faithfully through your every Jordan, right into your promised future.

> **God has already spoken everything pertaining to your success in life.**

When Christ was born, the group of singing angels,

who announced His arrival to the startled shepherds, declared God's peace and goodwill to all mankind in the precious gift of His Son, Jesus (Luke 2:14). In His official visit to Joseph, Gabriel told the soon-to-be husband and surrogate father that the holy Seed that was deposited in the womb of his betrothed virgin, shall be called Immanuel—God with us (Matthew 1:21). At the very onset, God was promising to be with all who would accept His Son as the Savior of the world. This promise is not different from the one He gave to Joshua as he stood before the mighty Jordan—"*the Lord your God is with you wherever you go*" (Joshua 1:9).

Such bright future

In the book of Jeremiah, the 29th chapter, God spoke a very precious promise to all His covenanted children. He said:

"*For I know the plans that I have for you,*" *declares the LORD,* "*plans for welfare and not for calamity <u>to give you a future and a hope.</u>* *¹²Then you will call upon Me and come and pray to Me, and I will listen to you.* *¹³You will seek Me and find Me when you search for Me with all your heart.*"

Jeremiah 29:11-13

The Word of God cannot be plainer. The Almighty already has a bright future, full of good hope, prepared for you. This future is already established and guaranteed because the words releasing it have already left the mouth of Jehovah.

God's word, spoken or written, will always succeed because it is powerful and enduring as His character. It is for this reason that Titus says it is totally impossible for God to tell a lie (Titus 1:2). Even if God were to try to lie, He couldn't—not only because He dwells in truth, but also because whatever escapes His lips becomes whatever He said. The wise King Solomon says that every word of God is tested—immaculately pure and flawless (Proverbs 30:5). David said that *"the words of the LORD are pure words; as silver tried in a furnace on the earth, refined seven times"* (Psalm 12:6). You can pledge your life and its future upon it.

Therefore, remember, whatever is yours by divine right can never be taken away from you by anyone but yourself. No one can curse you or remove God's blessing from you without your permission. If you fail to believe what God has spoken in His Word concerning you, and elect to meditate upon what others say about you, you will be opening the door for Satan to rob you of your blessings. Furthermore, if you choose to live in disobedience to the revealed will of God, as expressed in His living Word, you will shut yourself out from the future He has designed for you.

As I illustrated earlier in this chapter, the prophet Balaam could not curse whom God had blessed, nor could he turn back the future which God had spoken for the children of Israel. However, what King Balak could not accomplish through bribery, he was able to achieve through seduction, immorality and idolatry. He employed the beautiful women of his kingdom to lure the sons of Israel into harlotry and idol worship. Because of their sin and rebellion, the Israelites shut themselves out from God's favor and blessing and brought calamity and disaster upon their own heads. Had not Phinehas stood in the gap between the angry God and the whore-mongering congregation, many more than the 24,000 would have perished.

Since God has already spoken everything concerning you in His Word, your success or failure in this world is now left to you. No one, no government, no situation or circumstance has the power to nullify what God has already declared in His Word, or to stop you from achieving what He has already ordained for you. This is not just great news. This is a guaranteed future; and it was established even before your arrival into this sinful and very uncertain world. Under divine inspiration, David revealed this mysterious act of God for every life that comes into this world. He said:

¹⁶*Your eyes have seen my unformed substance; And in Your book were all written the days that were*

ordained for me, When as yet there was not one of them. *[17]How precious also are Your thoughts to me, O God! How vast is the sum of them!* *[18]If I should count them, they would outnumber the sand.*

Psalm 139:16-18

God saw your unformed substance—the blob of the fertilized egg—and wrote all your days, along with all His thoughts (or plans) for you, in His memory bank, even before the very first day of your existence. Such an understanding is so deep, David said, that our attempting to fathom everything about it is like us trying to count the grains of sand on the seashore. You see, dear reader, insofar as God is concerned, you existed in Him before you even came into this world, just as the design of a car, or anything else, exists in the mind of its creator before it appears as a finished product in the marketplace.

Nonetheless, with such a profound understanding of the Almighty and His spoken word, all that is left for you to do is to follow the instruction He has given through the prophet Jeremiah, and His servant Joshua. In Jeremiah He promises that if you seek him with all your heart, you will find Him, and when you call on Him in prayer, He will listen to you (Jeremiah 29:12, 13). Additionally, when you, like Joshua, are diligent in your obedience to all that God has revealed to you through your continuous meditation on His Word, He will empower you with His wisdom to make your way prosperous, and achieve *good* success.

Design Your Success

The story of Joshua makes it very evident that you do not only possess the capacity to position yourself for success in this world, but also the opportunity to shape the outcome of your future destiny. Just as God placed the responsibility upon Joshua to *make his [your] way prosperous and . . . have good success* (Joshua 1:8), so He is counting on you to cooperate with Him in bringing you into your appointed "Promise Land."

Notice that Joshua was the one making his way prosperous and his success good. God had spoken it, but Joshua was given the responsibility to produce it by diligently pursuing the instructions governing it in the Book of the Law. The situation is no different for you. Like Joshua, you too must make the most important decision of your life—that is, the commitment to surrender all of your life to the care of God and to all that He has written in His Word regarding human life on this planet. There is absolutely no getting around this, for the Almighty says that *"if you are willing and obedient, you will eat the good of the land"* (Isaiah 1:19).

155

The Word God would outlast and outclass any situation in your life.

The Word of the living God must become your un-contested life-long companion, counselor and guide. It must be the ultimate source of your reality for dealing with every situation in your life, regardless of how threatening; for the immortal, invisible, all-wise and almighty God stands back of every word that has proceeded from His mouth. God's Word is eternal and unchangeable as He Himself is. The Word, itself, says that He is the same *yesterday, today and forever* (Hebrews 13:8), and that He will not break His covenanted promises or alter any word that has gone out of His mouth (Psalm 89:34).

Whenever you choose to live by every word which proceeds from the mouth of God—reading, meditating, confessing and obeying its promises and precepts—that Word would outlast and outclass any situation in your life. Remember what Jesus said: *"Heaven and earth will pass away, but My words will not pass away"* (Matthew 24:35). It is easier for heaven and earth to pass away than for one word of God to fail.

God told Joshua to meditate upon the Word day and night so that he would be able to do all that was written in it. This is so essential for two very significant reasons—namely, (1) You will not know what is written in the Book, and especially things that pertain to your life and future success, if you fail to read the Book and meditate upon its very precious contents. (2) Through active, daily meditation on the Word of God, you will be programming your spirit and mind to think God's thoughts, so that you can both speak God's words and follow through with His guidance in your life. It is very difficult, nearly impossible, for someone to recognize the Spirit's leading if that individual is not immersed in, and governed by, the Word of God.

> **Good success is God-centered and stands aloof from the erosion produced by time and chance.**

True prosperity and *good* success come only to those who are willing to live by the conditions God laid down for their creation in His Word. *Good* success (Joshua 1:8) implies that there is also *bad* success. What makes the difference? The answer most certainly is the enduring presence of the eternal God. *Good* success is God-centered, and stands aloof from the erosion produced by time and chance, because it is produced by the eternal Word of the almighty God.

However, what the world frequently calls success often goes belly-up or turns into disaster when the world's systems, which support it, fail. Overnight the collapse of our current global economies devoured the prosperity and success that many thought would have provided them with future security. Many have committed suicide, while others totter precariously on the brink of financial disaster and complete disillusionment.

Currently, almost everyone is wary of all the man-made systems which purport the idea that they are the success vehicles for a secured future. People are holding on to their cash and other assets because they do not know whom to trust with them. Thank God, He is the most trustworthy Provider and Preserver in the entire universe! *Good* success comes only from Him, and only through Him. Such success involves the fulfillment of God's purpose for one's life in this world.

The Bible counsels, *"Put not your trust in princes, nor in the son of man in whom there is no help"* (Psalm 146:3). It also confirms, *happy is that people whose God is the Lord* (Psalm 144:15). As a matter of fact, in his very first psalm, David calls the individual blessed (or successful), who chooses not to walk in the counsel of the ungodly, nor "hang out" with sinners, nor keep company with scoffers; but, instead, that person delights in God's Word and meditates upon it day and night (Psalm 1:1, 2). Such a person, the rest of the psalm says, will live a life of prosperity and *good* success because God has already established the way for these to occur.

The end of your story

God has given you the precious privilege not only to position yourself for a successful future; but also the option of writing the end of your life-story. When Joshua wrote his, along with Israel's, he said:

"Now behold, today I am going the way of all the earth, and you know in all your hearts and in all your souls that not one word of all the good words which the LORD your God spoke concerning you has failed; all have been fulfilled for you, not one of them has failed."

Joshua 23:14

How do you want your story to end? That depends on how you plan to live the rest of your life, with its many Jordan crossings. Please consider the following as you contemplate your current situation and the future you envision for yourself.

1. Not one word of all the good words which the Lord your God has spoken concerning your life and future will fail.

2. Find those words that God has spoken concerning you; meditate upon them until they become a part of your thought-life and daily conversation.

159

3. Be determined to obey the Word to the very best of God's ability (your surrender). Do not turn from it (to the right or left) to follow your own reason or the thoughts of others.

4. Follow the promptings of your spirit, for the Spirit of God will guide you (Romans 8:16; 1 John 2:27). Measure every prompt and thought by what is already revealed in the Word. They must harmonize.

5. Be strong and very courageous, because God's got your back. He will never, ever fail you.

6. Live in expectation of success. Remember success is already given; just live in persistent pursuit of the conditions already established by God for its fulfillment. Make seeking the kingdom of God and the contents of His Word the top priority of your life (Matthew 6:33).

7. TESTIFY! Be very persistent in confessing God's Word (promises) on all your life's situations irrespective of what they present to you. One must give way—and that's not the Word, because it abides forever. Remember, not even one word which God has spoken concerning you will fail.

Child of the Most High God, position yourself for success. You've got what it takes to win—God Almighty and His unfailing Word! Open yourself to them in faith and obedience. Allow nothing and no one to distract or deter you from following all that the Father reveals to you in His Word. If you hold steadfastly to the Word, you will make your way prosperous and you will achieve *good success*; for God will fulfill His promise to bring you safely over your Jordans, and into the life He has designed for you.

About The Author

Dr. Ruthven Roy is the president of Network Discipling Connections, a discipling agency dedicated to the task of making, training and connecting disciples of Jesus for kingdom work around the world. He received his BA in Theology from the University of the Southern Caribbean, Master of Divinity and Doctor of Ministry degrees from Andrews University, and his Master of Business Administration from Western Michigan University. His experience as a teacher, pastor, evangelist and discipler spans a period of 36 years. Through his many seminars and workshops, Dr. Roy enjoys teaching and training believers how to become contagious, fruit-bearing Disciples of Jesus. He is also the author of five other compelling titles—A Challenge to the Remnant; The Explosive Power of Network Discipling; The Samson Xfile; Imitating God; Unshakeable Kingdom and Position Yourself for Success: God's Waiting to Do Wonders Through You. He and his wife, Lyris, have three adult daughters, Charisa, Lyrisa and Mirisa.

More Exciting Titles
by Dr. Ruthven J. Roy

The Samson Xfile

The Samson Xfile is the intriguing review of the most misunderstood faith-hero in the Bible—Samson. Christian tradition has perpetuated a negative view of this God-warrior; but the mysterious Xfile (Judges 14:4) of God's providence paints an amazingly very different picture. See your life reflected in God's dealing with Samson.

ISBN: 978-0-9717853-1-1 (Hardcover)
      978-0-9717853-2-8 (Paperback)

The Explosive Power of Network Discipling

"Every Christian is called to be a disciple of Jesus; and every disciple is called to be a fisher, not just a member!" In this volume Dr. Roy clearly explains Christ's master plan for growing His kingdom. Christ calls everyone to discipleship, not membership.

ISBN: 978-0-9717853-4-2

Imitating God

Imitating God is not only possible, but it is also guaranteed. This book will make available to you the key to your true identity, and will show you, in very simple steps, how to unleash the power of God's life from within you. Get ready to enter into the **God-zone.**

ISBN: 978-0-9717853-3-5

Study Guide: Imitating God

Do not forget this companion Study Guide to go along with this magnificent text. It would greatly enhance your understanding of all the vital issues that pertain to your spiritual identity and living victoriously. Moreover, this Study Guide will provide you with an exciting, hands-on way to share this good news with others.

ISBN: 978-0-9717853-6-6

Unshakeable Kingdom

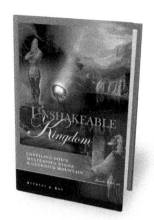

In the church, yet outside God's kingdom! What a tragedy! Learn how to avoid the "Nicodemus Syndrome," the common sickness of modern Christianity! Understand true kingdom fitness and why religion is simply not enough. *The kingdom of heaven is NOW; not later! Later is TOO late!* This volume will change your focus and your life in a way that only a miracle from God can. *Seize the moment, and make the decision to enter God's Unshakeable Kingdom now!*

ISBN: 978-0-9717853-3-5

Available at your local Christian bookstore

For more information, visit www.networkdiscipling.org, or write to Rehoboth Publishing, P.O. Box 33, Berrien Springs, MI 49103

Contact Information

Dr. Ruthven J. Roy

NETWORK DISCIPLING MINISTRIES
P.O. Box 33
Berrien Springs, MI 49103

Tel: (301) 514-2383
Email: ruthvenroy@networkdiscipling.org
Website: www.networkdiscipling.org

CPSIA information can be obtained
at www.ICGtesting.com
Printed in the USA
FFHW01n2208310718
47598247-51108FF